"Tom Center's book is interesting to me because I had an uncle who was in Vietnam. Tom's book has details that go beyond the movies and most books because it is written about everyday experiences with a fresh description. Most books are written from memories. This is everyday existence. You experience the tragedies from the letters home to the thoughts captured in print. This book is engrossing and hard to put down."

—Tim Head,
Vietnam vet's nephew, Bible study enthusiast

"A very moving, well-written story. It meant a lot to read about the war by one of the heroes who was actually involved. A special God bless you to Tom for helping me understand this part of our history. Our generation gave so much. Thank God Tom did make it home. Reading his story is helping me deal with my own guilt—he had to go, and I didn't. Also, I don't think I really understood all Tom went through. I am proud that I have had the honor to know Tom Center. Everyone should read the book and feel what the war was like for the young men there. Life is stranger than fiction. Tom's writing means so much to me and to many other people. His writing is so powerful."

—Karen Firth Howard,
Relative, friend, and classmate of
numerous combat veterans

"This book is a paradoxical mix of easy-to-read yet powerful messages of earthly struggles being overcome with hope. I highly recommend it."

—Kent Killebrew,
Director of quality assurance, food industry

"I enjoyed every word of this book. Tom did a great job. Well-written and nicely told. The style is reminiscent of *The Things They Carried*. I like the back and forth between battle and Tom's personal feelings and insights gained through that experience. There's a lot of meat in his insights. This book should enjoy a wide audience. There is a lot of interest in the Vietnam era among young people, and vets are a strong reading group. Of my 14 novels, the Vietnam novels have been the best, largely due to Vietnam vets and the children of vets. Their comments have been very rewarding. I'll be one of Tom's first customers."

—Raymond Hunter Pyle,
Author of numerous books

"I enjoyed reading *The CrossRoads Diaries*. Tom's writing has a transparent honesty along with an immediacy that makes it seem not so long ago. The photos were helpful; they corrected mistaken notions of what the gunboats were. Tom captured emotions well, from being under fire to idly writing, as well as figuring out life as a young man. Thank you, Tom, for this book, for recording things so well, and for now being willing to share this with others. I hope that your sharing and the Patriotic Program of the College of the Ozarks will bring healing to other veterans. And thank you for your love for the Lord. I hope that I might see you again soon."

—Stanley W. Schultz, Jr.,
Pastor and counselor of PTSD veterans

The CrossRoads Diaries **Facebook page public domain comments:**

Sandra C. – "It is a story of truth and survival and of the Lord's protection and blessings."

Jack V. – "This memoir is a captivating man on the ground, or rather water, account of what life was like in America's 'brown water navy,' the Riverine Force. Through vivid storytelling and original images, Tom's tale of his experiences in the Vietnam War are [sic] presented in an intimate way often missing from the narrative of this tumultuous time in American history."

Steve R. – "It's a wonderful book. Once I began reading it, I was unable to put it down even though it was after midnight. The music he quotes were songs that I grew up with and fit very smoothly into the narrative he was creating. Men like Mr. Center should be honored for their service."

Mary J. – "Tom, I just finished your book. So moving and well-written. Thank you for sharing everything. It was fascinating."

Bonnie A. – "What a journey!"

THE CrossRoads DIARIES

A 19-YEAR-OLD'S VIETNAM JOURNEY

TOM CENTER

CLAY BRIDGES
PRESS

Table of Contents

This book is dedicated to my cousin Billy—Bill Ammons, Jr. He is the one who heard all the stories in one night. It is also dedicated to the boys (men) of the Mekong Delta who lived the stories. And last, but not least, it is dedicated to my wife who has survived the repercussions of these stories.

Life is just a story
We sing while we live.
It may be full of grief or glory,
But it's nothing until we give.

The flag in the background flew on Tango 91–4 until August 16, 1968.

Foreword

In 1967, the Beatles released their iconic *Sgt. Pepper's Lonely Hearts Club Band* album. The final track was "A Day in the Life." In the pages that follow, you will be taken on a year-in-the-life journey through the Mekong Delta of South Vietnam alongside a sailor of the unique Army-Navy combat unit known as the Mobile Riverine Force, with 19-year-old Tom Center as your guide.

I first met Tom in March 2016 in the Springfield-Branson (Missouri) National Airport terminal just a couple of hours prior to our departure to Vietnam on a patriotic education trip sponsored by the College of the Ozarks where I have taught for more than 30 years. By all outward appearances, Tom fit the stereotypical image of a Vietnam vet who was still living in (or reliving) the 1960s. His long hair held in place by a bandana and flowing grayish beard were easy marks that set him apart from others in the Ozarks, a very conservative region of the country. When I approached Tom to introduce myself, I could see a twinkle in his eyes and a grin that indicated that life had changed for him, even if his hairstyle had not. I sensed this man had a story to tell, and over the next two weeks of our trip and in the years since, I have been able to peel back several layers of his complicated personal saga. Tom's journey interested me because I not only teach a course on the Vietnam War but on the year 1968 as well.

Tom enlisted in the Navy in 1967 and volunteered for combat duty in South Vietnam. He went to war to die, but while he was in the country, he decided he wanted to live. Tom was a radioman on an armored troop carrier, part of River Assault Division 91. His boat was Tango 91-4, the Delta Queen. During his first tour, Riverine Tango

91-4 patrolled the murky waters of the Mekong Delta, often taking enemy fire at the intersection of rivers and canals called the Crossroads, or Ambush Alley. But there is much more to *The CrossRoads Diaries* than just the Viet Cong entrapment. Along the way, the reader will be introduced to Roger-Dodger, Frank, Robert, and Larry (aka, Gomer), who were Tom's brothers in arms. You will also meet Jacquie, someone Tom had known since the sixth grade and who will become his reason for surviving the war. After all, anyone who decides to buy an engagement ring rather than saving money for a Datsun 240Z must have thought she was someone special. You will read letters to and from Tom's mother. Some of the letters are amusing, such as Tom asking for Baby Ruth candy bars and a subscription to *Reader's Digest,* and some of the letters will tug at the heart as his mother seeks to comfort and reassure her son that someone at home still cares, loves, and prays for him daily.

The CrossRoads Diaries is a mixture of poetry, pictures, Bible scripture, and musical lyrics, but most of all, it is the innermost feelings, the actual diary of a young man who spent more than 300 hours per month on river operations in the Mekong Delta, was in more than 100 firefights, earned a Purple Heart courtesy of the Viet Cong, and came home only to return for a second tour as a minesweeper on the Cua Viet River just south of the DMZ (demilitarized zone). This work is in the same genre as Philip Caputo's *A Rumor of War* or Tim O'Brien's *The Things They Carried*, but in many ways, it is more personal, which makes it appealing.

I cannot begin to understand everything the Mobile Riverine Force had to endure in 1967 and 1968, not the least of which was the Tet Offensive. But I am so very grateful to know Tom Center because even after three decades of collegiate teaching, I am still a student of history, and I am still learning about American involvement in Vietnam. Who better to be my teachers than the soldiers who fought and lived through the war? There was a time not that long ago when Vietnam vets were shamed, shunned, and demonized. Thankfully, time has healed many of the country's wounds, and one by one, those who wore our nation's uniform are now receiving the respect and gratitude they so richly deserve. Welcome home, Tom. It has been my honor and privilege to travel with you, to know you, and most of all, to call you my friend.

—C. David Dalton, PhD
Elizabeth Hoyt Clark, Chair of Humanities and
Professor of History, College of the Ozarks

A Short History of the Mobile Riverine Force

I t is easy to imagine a child asking a combat veteran sailor or soldier a simple question such as, "What did you do in the war?" The answer might be, "Oh, I just rode a boat on the river." But riding a boat on a river in the Mekong Delta of Vietnam was not a pleasure cruise. For a sailor, it was similar to being part of the PT boats of World War II and the misfits of the TV show *McHale's Navy* and all the while being somewhat like an infantryman. For a soldier, it would be a daily event to do combat amphibious assault landings such as D-Day and living like naval Marines of the seventeenth and eighteenth centuries.

The statistics of mass shootings in America between 1966 and 2018 are substantial. But in the two years of the existence of the Mobile Riverine Force (MRF), the statistics for firefights far exceed the combined totals of those mass shootings. The Riverine participants and victims also had the responsibilities of first responders, situational event cleanup, and immediate readiness to deal with it again.

The unique concept of an MRF combat unit lay dormant for more than a century. The first Mobile Riverine Force consisted of an Army and Navy cooperation during the US Civil War in which General Ulysses S. Grant loaded 32,000 Union soldiers onto riverboats to begin the siege of the Confederate city of Vicksburg, Virginia. Grant's Army forces teamed up with Admiral Porter's Navy forces to carry the North's offensive deep into the South. The Navy provided armor-protected boats along with fire support to safely and efficiently deliver the Army troops to their places of battle. Volleys of cannon fire, rifles, and mortars from the naval gunships greatly aided the North. Riverine warfare virtually split the Confederacy in two.

The twentieth-century Mobile Riverine Force, the likes of which had not been seen since Grant's forces, consisted of US Army infantry of the 9th Division accompanied by the Navy's Task Force 117. Instead of the muddy banks of the Mississippi River, the MRF now found itself in the muddy waters of the Mekong Delta, which extends from the Tibetan Plateau to the South China Sea. The MRF was reinstalled for similar reasons to those for which it had been created in the 1800s—to move combat forces into the 26,000 square miles of the Viet Cong stronghold and sanctuary in the Mekong. General William Westmoreland borrowed from the tactical forces of the campaign in the Mississippi along with the expertise of the French naval assault during the Indochina War to revolutionize what came to be known as riverine warfare and requested that such a force once more be created.

This second Mobile Riverine Force in US military history proved itself to be an effective means of searching the Mekong Delta in pursuit of the Viet Cong. The new force was formed in June 1967 based on the concepts used in the Mississippi Delta campaign during the Civil War. Vietnam's forces consisted of air, artillery, and infantry elements of the 9th Division that were aided by the gunboats and ships of the US Navy River Assault Flotilla ONE. Riding the boats in the Delta was one of the most dangerous duties during the Vietnam War.

Bombardment of Island "Number Ten" in the Mississippi River, April 7, 1862, by Currier & Ives, New York. Courtesy Naval History and Heritage Command National Archives – KN-969.

The Mobile Riverine Force flagship *USS Benewah,* the most decorated ship of the Vietnam War. Courtesy Naval History and Heritage Command National Archives – USN 1142271.

Introduction

The title of the book, *The CrossRoads Diaries*, has significant meanings. "Cross" is for the One who saves us all, and "Roads" represents the paths we travel. "Diaries" represent a written record of what has occurred at a place and time that may include emotions and reflections. We all encounter crossroads in our lives. Crossroads is a place of decision because there are several paths we can take. We can go straight, left, or right, or we can turn around and try to go back where we came from. The Crossroads in the Mekong Delta of Vietnam was a nickname for a difficult place for the Mobile Riverine Force. It was an intersection of a river and a canal situated between My Tho and Ben Tre and known for hundreds of firefights.

Join me, a Berkeley, California, native (raised in Riverside, California), who at the age of 18 volunteered to serve in Vietnam for the sole purpose of dying in a blaze of glory. Read the firsthand account of how a lost soul seeking death experiences firefights, unimaginable losses, and combat injuries to discover the gift of life. I have had many requests during the past 50 years to tell about my time in Vietnam. December 1967 marked the beginning of my first tour in Vietnam. That tour is captured in this book, *The CrossRoads Diaries*. Near the end of the book are a few incidents that occurred in March 1970 during my second tour in Vietnam. All comments directly relating to the Bible are derived from the King James Version.

In this book, I have faced the demons and the blessings; the good, the bad, and the ugly; the right and the wrong; and the exhilarating experiences of being a young man in combat. There were choices I made that affected many people. Memories fade and get distorted by life's events. I have no intention to deceive, manipulate, avoid, or change anything that occurred. As Si Robertson of *Duck Dynasty* fame stated, "It is mostly truthful."

This book was written for the following:

- Veterans, to let them know there is always hope in the future despite the horrors of the past
- Those seeking knowledge of what combat situations can create in the physical world but also in a person's mental and emotional being
- Young people who are experiencing the initial changes from childhood to adulthood
- Parents and significant others of combat service members who are seeking insights about their loved ones
- Anyone wanting to know a little bit about one of the most unique combat units that ever existed

1967 Prologue

Spring 1967

Spring is the time of new life. Eggs hatch, and growth begins. Boot camp is over, and it is a time to enjoy life in San Diego. I am away from home and on my own. Sorta! Mom had to sign for me to join the Navy because I was so young, and she did so on the expectation I would not have to go to Vietnam. The only things I knew about Vietnam were that it was a place far away, some Army guys were going there to fight, and a few were losing their lives. Many parents were concerned that their sons would be drafted and then killed in Vietnam. I didn't understand anything about something called the Gulf of Tonkin incident and the Tonkin Gulf Resolution that allowed the president to escalate the number of US service members being sent to that faraway place.

Although unauthorized, four guys decide to share an apartment so the time can be more enjoyable. The apartment has a small bed, one sofa sleeper, and a tiny kitchen with a dining table. It is across the street from the San Diego Zoo. Put a uniform on, and you get in for free. Still a virgin but getting tested to the max. Still a total abstainer but succumbs at a party to celebrate the end of our off-duty living arrangement. How would I know that a Michelob would taste like vanilla ice cream? I had to scream, "Give me mo!" Oh, that Michelob! In a day or so, off I go to a city by the bay all because of a decision on a very fateful day.

"The Summer of Love"

Jerry and some of his friends plus Grace and some of her friends, all musicians, do free music gigs in the big park. Trolleys, unusual aromas, Haight-Ashbury, flowers, and living on an island in the middle of the bay provide a unique living situation. Who is 18 years old and doesn't want to be in San Francisco during the summer of '67? Me! I love being here. I just don't want to be alive! I DON'T WANT TO BE ALIVE! I have cut off my relationship with the one who tried to seduce me in San Diego. Suicide seems like a good idea, but it would embarrass the family. I will purposely flunk out of electronics school and go commit suicide in a blaze of glory fighting in Vietnam.

In a few months, Country Joe and the Fish will be singing my theme song about moms packing their boys off to Vietnam and dads not hesitating to send sons off before it's too late. The song exclaims,

"Be the first one on your block, to have your boy come home in a box."

So I study real hard, don't want any accidental mistakes. I flunked the big exam and get sent to personnel, and then they asked where I want to go. "I want to go to Vietnam and be on a gunboat." "*We can sign you up for an ATC.*" "What's that?" "*Don't know.*" "Okay by me." "*Sign the bottom line,*" and then there's no turning back!

The Fall of 1967, S.E.R.E., and the 50-Cal.

Let's go to Whidbey Island, Washington, and be miserable. Let's learn about Survival Evasion Resistance and Escape. Let's not eat hardly anything for a week, forget about sleeping, and there is so much more fun we're going to have. We will be able to rappel down a cliff and grab quarter-sized crabs to snack on, fresh from the sea to our mouths with a tasty little crunch (partly because of the sand). Don't forget about the random green blackberries or Charlie (he's a cross between "Big Bad John" the song and basketball player Lew Alcindor of UCLA fame), tying a bayonet to a stick, chasing down a skinny little rabbit, skinning it, and making a stew with seawater to feed about 10 to 12 of us guys (the only meal we had that week). After we hide for a while, we will get to be captured and spend some time as POWs. We get to spend time in a box where you can't lie down or stand up or even really sit. Lying on a slanted downward board with water being poured on your face keeps you from getting bored. Staying at a camp flying the flag of the Viet Cong for a week ends at sunrise time with their flag being replaced by our flag. Everyone has a tear in their eye to see the Stars and Stripes flying in the sky.

The 50-caliber machine gun is a fascinating weapon. Every boat has several of them, and everyone must know how to shoot them, clear a jam, and do a field strip. Field strip: take it apart, then lay it out for inspection, and put it all back together properly—in the dark, lights off, except for the inspections.

Back to being prepared for survival, the swimming lessons must be mentioned. Jump into the Olympic size pool and go the length of it and then back to the start point. Easier said than done. When you start to jump, you are told what two limbs of your four that you can't use, and you can't make any ripples or noises. Wish my friend Charlie had learned that better and wasn't so afraid of the water.

Dec 11, 1967

It's been fun with a lot of it being in the Bay Area since this past spring. That was one cold-hearted emotionless typewritten letter you sent to Jacquie who tried so hard to seduce you. You did try hard to unite with that cute blonde ponytail young lady from high school, but it didn't work out. Spending a few weekend nights at the Fillmore listening to music by The Doors was fantastic, but now it's time to go to war.

So who is going with you?

There's Roger, known as Roger-Dodger, some kind of weird version of Roger, over and out. He's my age but from a different world, not the youth-oriented pace of Southern Cal but that down-home style of the South, hard-working, tough times, he's already married, and they are expecting their first child soon. He's been having a rough time of making ends meet with the small Navy paycheck. The best way to increase the amount he gets is to volunteer for combat duty, so he's going to war.

Rodger-Dodger had a self-made tattoo,
The letters of which were only a few.
There was a big "M" and a big "O"
In Hawaii that would be "mo"
And mean there is certainly more,
But the final "M" proved too sore!

There is Frank from San Diego. His dad was a twenty-year man in the Navy. Frank knows he must serve his time in the military. The Reserves provide the shortest time of actual commitment. A great way to shorten it, even a little bit more, is to volunteer for Vietnam. He and his dad have had many arguments about the whole situation. Nonetheless, Frank and his camera are going to war.

There is Robert. He has always wanted to be a policeman, but driving the Admiral's craft wasn't doing much to prepare him for his future, and in one and a half years, he will need more experience in the ways a cop has to think and react. One way to get that experience is to drive boats in the Delta. He made a formal request and finally was called into the Admiral's office. The high-ranking officer informed Robert that his orders had come through. Robert will get to face all the fears and hardships of war. He will be the cox'n of an assault boat in the Mekong Delta. By law he's not even a man yet until he turns 21 in a month or so. Robert is going to war.

There is Larry. But no one knows him by that name. Somehow, someway, he picked up the nickname Gomer. He is known for drunkenness, whores, fights, and gambling. After some kind of binge, he found himself in front of a ship's captain where he was about to receive a period of confinement but was offered a second chance. He would be sentenced to a term of hard labor, or he could choose a new assignment, an assignment that had him going to war. There are two others in this initial seven-man crew, but they will remain nameless due to life events. A year from now, when we return, there will be 11 of us boarding the plane, and other survivors may have left at different times. There are now a few more than 120 leaving for Vietnam, and our unit will experience an 80% casualty rate during the next year.

Our first stop today will be in Hawaii. We will get off the plane for a little while and be able to use the restroom. As I stand at my urinal relieving myself, someone calls my name. The person to my right is a Navy officer in his whites, including his white buck shoes. I turn to respond to the calling, and my yellow stream hits his white shoes. He wasn't very happy. What's the worst he can do to me? Send me to war?

Here begins the diary from the memory of a young man in Vietnam.

⊕ ⊕ ⊕

Dec 13, 1967 – Goood Morning, Vietnam!

We arrived last night after a very long flight.
You look around left and then to the right.
The French influence can easily be seen
In bright colors of red, blue, yellow, and green.
I look at my hands with scores of mosquito bites.
Glad I slept in my uniform buttoned up tight.
The aromas are nasty and foul to the senses,
December heat and humidity gives us glimpses
Of the life that is about to be
While fighting for others to be free.
I have no regrets about coming to this place,
Just a little edgy about what I will face.
I'll be home by Christmas of next year,
It's how I'll get there that I fear.
Mom and others are praying to God to hold me safely
While on the rivers as His grace flows so freely.
How am I to know what He has in store?
Will I want for less or be wanting more?

Frank from San Diego took a snapshot of me just after we
woke up on the first morning of our year in Vietnam.

8

Dec 15, 1967 – Dong Tam
(Vietnamese - United Hearts and Minds)

Well it's about time to leave Saigon, thank goodness. It has been several days of dealing with REMFs so we can go be the FNGs. The mosquito bites, all 40+ of them, are starting to heal, and it is now time to gather up my luggage and head into the Delta. I really don't understand why I brought a duffle bag, two suitcases, and two weekend travel bags full of stuff. Where do I think I'm going, and how am I going to use what I have brought?

The five of us plus two others and the rest of the class we trained with jump on board an Army transport cargo plane. We go on a short southwest flight to a place called Dong Tam. It is the Army base for the 9th Infantry Division who supplies the combat troops for the combat boats we will be on. As we start to descend, the pilot makes an announcement that we are landing on a helicopter landing strip, and he only wants to touch down and immediately take off. He says he is tired of being shot at when he flies to this place. He lands, stops, we jump off, he takes off—120 plus guys with their luggage exit a plane that landed and flew away in less than one minute.

With minimal introduction to where we are and what we will be doing, we are delivered to our riverine boats. My fellow crewmen and I are taken to Tango 91-four, or T-91-4, Tango Four, Dragonfly Tango Four (radio call sign). We are a subdivision of River Squadron 9 (RivRon 9), River Division 91 (RivDiv 91). Tango Four is an Armored Troop Carrier, or ATC.

This boat is definitely not a peacetime pleasure cruise craft. It was originally an LCM (World War II Landing Craft Medium as seen in the movies about D-Day). It can carry a small tank or about a platoon of soldiers. It has 1-inch steel plating all around its modified superstructure and has been modified to include substantial armament. In the well deck are four 30-caliber machine guns, each with approximately 3,000 rounds of belted ammunition. Up topside on the port and starboard just behind the cox'n flat (boat driver box) are two 50-caliber machine guns with grenade launchers on them. The boat captain sits outside between the two machine gun mounts behind the cox'n flat and in front of the 20-mm cannon (sometimes considered the largest type of machine gun). Inside the cox'n flat are two shotguns, two M16s, two 38-caliber revolvers, two 45-caliber semiautomatic handguns (M1911), and various other odds and ends of handguns, knives, and such. The boat also carries a stock of C-4 explosives, resupply ammunition for the Army and our guns, several hundred cases of combat rations, and medical supplies, including any and all the morphine we want anytime we want it.

Here is what we don't have: running water, bathroom, and cooking facilities. We do have a bucket to get river water for our bucket toilet, bucket sink, and bucket shower. A used C-rat (combat rations) can and a C-4 are great for cooking. There are four folddown canvas cots for sleeping. That's plenty because someone has to be awake 24/7, and the boat is always running in case we need to get underway instantly. But don't think about fast getaways. The boat is so big and heavy that it has a battle speed of 8 knots, and going that fast (?) will blow the engines. Sometimes, when it's raining heavily and the tide is going out, the Mekong River and tributaries can flow at 10 miles per hour. If you're trying to go upstream, you're not.

All the converted LCMs have an enclosable cox'n flat for the driver and the radioman. The well deck on the boat serves as a waterborne Greyhound bus for soldiers, and it is also the living room, dining room, and bedroom for the crew.

The cox'n flat with steel plates and bar armor down

Tango boats

Dec 16, 1967 – More Boat Info

My river division is also known as RAD 91. That's short for River Assault Division 91. I have thrown away most of the stuff I brought. It just wouldn't fit into the tiny locker aboard this boat. It reminds me of the PE locker at Rubidoux High School where you put your street clothes during class time. We have already discovered that you can put C-rat cans on the boat engines, and they will be warm enough to eat in about one hour.

Besides the ATCs, we have boats named Monitors, similar to that Civil War boat we learned about in high school. It does not have a well deck for carrying troops but instead has a recessed area for an 81 mm mortar and at the front of the boat a 40 mm cannon. Speaking of 40 mm, I forgot to mention there are two grenade handguns in the cox'n flat called bloopers, and the mounted ones on the 50-caliber machine guns are hand crank grenade launchers. The rate of fire is the rate of crank. You can fire machine guns and grenade launchers at the same time. The new monitors will be arriving soon, and instead of the 40 mm cannon, it will have a 105 Howitzer with a sawed-off barrel. Its primary round is called a beehive that sends out darts that will pin people to trees.

RivDiv 91 monitor and command boat

The monitors are considered our battleship, and we also have what we call our aircraft carrier. The ATC(H) is an assault craft that has a helicopter landing pad mounted on it. The pad is so small that the pilot is unable to see it as he does a touchdown. This craft is used for medical evacuations and has a miniature hospital emergency room underneath the pad.

We have a few other assorted boats. One is called an ASPB (Alpha Boat), and another is called a Zippo. The ASPB is our fastest boat and can zigzag and quickly provide additional fire support, but it's also more vulnerable to the enemy. The Zippo boat is named after the Zippo lighter but not because it can shoot fire, Napalm type. It is because it takes a Zippo lighter to light the fire that it shoots (read that a few times, and you'll understand).

Irma la Douche—not just the name of a boat; it's a type of boat. A Douche boat carries a water cannon and supports the Zippos in clearing the riverbanks but not in the way that immediately springs to mind. The water cannons are capable of 3,000 psi and are used to

Our aircraft carrier

13

drown tunnels and literally wash away riverside bunkers. This may seem a strange weapon, but some of the mud bunkers are capable of withstanding 105 mm bombardment with ease, yet all fall before the water jet of the Douche boats.

ASPB (Alpha Boat). Courtesy Naval History and Heritage Command National Archives – USN 1132289.

Zippo—Got a light, buddy? Courtesy Naval History and Heritage Command National Archives – K-84314.

Douche boat. Courtesy Naval History and Heritage Command National Archives – K-69363.

Every boat has a name, just like the planes and tanks in WW II and other combat situations. Our boat has been renamed the *Delta Queen*, probably because so many of us have a Southern background. We know that name represents a boat of the South in any of the many deltas and rivers that are part of that US territory. Frank might have been happier with one of the other boats with a new name, like the one called the Rubber Cookie, a take-off on the Beatles' album *Rubber Soul*. I am sure he will be hanging out with that boat crew quite a bit.

In a few days, there will be the ceasefire truce so we can have a peaceful Christmastime.

This will be an interesting year.

Dec 18, 1967 – First Letter

I am sure some of my diary entries and letters home will not always perfectly match up. As any police officer will tell you, the memories and reality get confused, especially when you purposely leave information out or choose to mislead when writing home. John is my brother.

Dear Family,

Well, I've been here in Vietnam for a week. I still haven't written. It hasn't really been because of neglect. I just have been unable because of all kinds of crazy reasons. Today is the first day that I have been with my gear and still have to relax. So far, I find this place most enjoyable. The weather is perfect, mid 80s during the day and in the low 60s at night. I'm stationed aboard an air-conditioned ship but find it just as comfortable sleeping on the boat. The boat is some machine.

You wouldn't believe the amount and variety of guns. The boat's name is *Delta Queen*. The last two weeks have been most interesting. That last week at Mare Island was something else. And the last weekend with Stephanie was most enjoyable. Oh, by the way, I gave her my green sweater to save for me and a couple of shirts. I think she might be coming by sometime after Christmas. If and when she does, I told her she could use my pea coat for a year, and she could have any of my shirts in the closet.

I got the chance to see Saigon during the daytime and at night. What a town! From Saigon, we flew to Dong Tam. I don't really know exactly where that's at, but it is south of Saigon. The plane's landing is something to remember. It landed on a helicopter landing strip, and the pilot was scared of being trapped in a firefight, so it was a very fast landing. I could be coming home sometime around the 10th of December. But that's a while off yet. Would you please help me spread my address around, like put it in the church bulletin? And John, be sure to give it to any pretty girl you know or meet or just happen to pass by.

I can't think of anything for you to send me, but if you do, don't feel shy about sending it. Well, I've got to go and write about a dozen letters. Bye for now.

Love,
Tom

Dec 20, 1967 – Work It Out!

Here we are, the five of us plus two more. We have our assigned positions on this craft of destruction. Robert is the driver, known as a cox'n, which is short for coxswain, a Navy term for boat driver. Gomer is the engineman, and he keeps the boat running. He also will be responsible for shooting four different machine guns, and he will shoot all four at the same time. There is Frank who is on one 50-caliber machine gun mount, and there's Roger-Dodger up on the 20-millimeter cannon. One guy is the other 50-caliber gunner, and one is the boat captain. That leaves me, but what am I? Who am I? I am known as the radioman. I maintain the communication between us and the world around us. I am a kid in a man's world, and I am a man in an unknown world. Talking on the radio sounds simple enough, but it is time to add a major multiple Catch 22. Daily life on the boat is noisy, and being in a gun battle is noisier. We have headsets and microphones available so we can talk to each other like they do in those planes in war movies. I have a headset with earphones and a microphone for talking on three different radios. I was never trained on how to talk on all of them at the same time. Only moms know how to talk to three people (kids) at the same time and understand all conversations. Let's talk about the radios. With a total of three, I need to monitor or talk with our River Division boats, the River Squadron commander, supplemental boats, the Army unit we are supporting, the support units who are supporting us, the support units who are supporting the Army, including helicopters (Army and Navy), planes (Army and Navy), artillery units, and even Navy ships. The math of multiple headsets and people to communicate with far outnumbers the boat or this radioman's capabilities. "If you don't want to work, you shouldn't hire on." It is just about time for us to go to work.

You do what you have to do to get done what needs to be done.
It doesn't matter if it's fun, Why walk when you can run!
And "Don't take a knife to a gunfight!
Win, and then decide who is right.

Dec 22, 1967 – First Operation

We have just got back from our first operation. It started on the 20th of December, and today is the 22nd. Three river division groups of boats along with three infantry battalions have been out and about looking for Charlie (that's what we call the VC—Viet Cong—the enemy). A RivDiv 111 (RAD111) Alpha boat (ASPB) hit a mine. That boat had a crew of five. Three got wounded, and one lost his life. Charlie avoided direct contact with the Riverine forces.

We did get to practice a little bit of shooting because we were in a free-fire zone. That kind of location is where you can shoot when you want whether or not you are being shot at. Gomer demonstrated how he could get all four machine guns shooting. We have been told to only shoot a few sporadic rounds at a time unless you have a direct target, but that was not the way Gomer did it. Gomer knew that if he shot several hundred rounds continuously until the barrel got extremely hot, the weapon would fire without the trigger being pulled. That's called cook-off rounds. Have you ever seen four machine guns firing without anyone controlling them? It's a strange sight because the barrels fly around in any direction they can. Of course, afterward the barrels have to be thrown away and then replaced. We have plenty of spare barrels for all weapons.

Dec 24, 1967 – Christmas Eve Day

Yesterday, we cleaned up the mud and the muck that the troops had deposited on and in our boat. We also resupplied all the ammunition that we had enjoyably used, cleaned our weapons, loaded up on fuel, and generally prepared to go out again.

We have been told that we're headed to a place the combat veterans refer to as The Crossroads. It has a second name, Ambush Alley, because of the numerous firefights that have occurred in that vicinity. We have been given orders to implement the Christmas Truce Operation. From the official summary report, "The enemy responded with small arms fire on occasions during the day. Fires were returned by Army and Navy units with unknown results." Someone forgot to mention that the enemy also fired a few rockets at us. The official document of this day claims there was only a minor skirmish with the enemy. Minor is a rather relative term for the first time you experience a gun battle. Someone in our group of boats clicked the talk button of his radio microphone as gunfire was exchanged and screamed, "I just crapped in my pants." How do I write home about that? I don't know. I just know it's a Silent Night.

Silent Night

Silent Night – The night might be quiet but the day not so much. There was gunfire, explosions, yelling, and such.

Holy Night – It is now Sunday and Christmas Eve, and from this war supposedly a reprieve.

All is calm – We are to halt their movement on the ground, but we know they're scurrying all around.

All is bright – We see the flares shot into the night to change the darkness into light.

Round yon virgin – To be pure and innocent is now lost, and it has come at a cost.

Mother and child – Many have wanted the comfort of mom to give them assurance and be calm.

Holy infant so tender and mild – We have started our journey into war, and I know we'll be shaken to our core.

Sleep in heavenly peace.

Sleep in heavenly peace.

Dec 25, 1967 – Second Letter to Home

Hi folks & John,   ② Christmas Day

Well, today is the day. Its a nice day here. Sun is shinning bright, sky clear & blue, pretty warm, but its been hotter. Slept until 8 this morning, had a nice breakfast & shower, clean the boat, and slept again. Just finish my turkey dinner (lunch) Sound nice doesn't it. Well it is, but to be more specific we're out an an operation have been for 2 days, and still another to go. I slept until 8 because before going to be bed I had been up 38 hrs out of 40. Breakfast consisted of turkey, fruit cocktail, and chocholate milk. The shower was 4 of us washing each other with buckets of water from the river. And lunch was a C-ration like breakfast. But to be truthful, I don't mind, its different and

I JUST FOUND OUT SOMETHING, …NEVER VOLUNTEER FOR OBSERVATION DUTY!

PAVLA ©1966

I kind of like it.

Thank you for sending my Dress Blues. As it turn out I needed them. They're stored away right now. I'm not hunting for food around this place, I've yet to be hungry since arriving. When we're moored along the ship we're assigned, life is pretty good, plenty of hot & cold water, air condition spaces, movies, free laundry, free hair cuts, but there's always a little bit of work to be done on the boat. I don't have a lot of free time, but I'm not hurting from it.

This was the only stationary around at it time, its not the best but it works. I have enclosed a list of things which would make life a little more enjoyable. I haven't got much more to say, so bye for now—

Love
Tom

SUPPLY DEPT.

PAULA

GREETINGS!
...FROM ONE OF YOUR
MISFIT FRIENDS!

1. Green Levies (waist 30, no length, it doesn't matter)
2. Instant Ice Tea (prefered with Lemon added)
3. Peanuts (like cashews)
4. Candy bars (Baby Ruths)
5. any thing else you would like to send, but don't over do yourself trying to send me any everything I want. It would send you to the poor house.

I ALWAYS HEARD AN ARMY MOVED ON ITS STOMACH!

Dec 29, 1967 – That's Ugly

Well, we got through the truce operation. Charlie did try to give us some Christmas presents on Christmas Day, but his deadly little presents were pesky fleas compared to the wasps, hornets, and insect bombs we gave back to him. Ours were bigger, badder, and fully outnumbered anything he could have possibly wanted. We got back to our base on the 26th and did the cleanup and resupply drill. Yesterday, the 28th, we set sail again to this place known as Snoopy's Nose.

The Rach Ba Rai River, better known as Snoopy's Nose, is where Tango 91-4 had a disastrous encounter with the enemy on September 15, 1967. It was a two-day battle where three sailors were killed and 61 wounded. We heard about it when we were training.

We were not trained for what we saw today. It is one of the ugliest water-land crafts that could possibly exist anywhere at any time. It is called a Pac-Vee, PACV or Patrol Air Cushion Vehicle (hovercraft). It can flow over land or water at more than 60 knots per hour, but you can hear it coming from a long way off. I just wonder what nonmilitary usages it might have. Maybe someday we will find out, but I don't think it's going to be a very useful combat piece of equipment. The VC has given it a name—Monster. We will be with this monster until the end of this year. Then what?

PACV. Courtesy Naval History and Heritage Command National Archives –
K-33308.

New Year's Day, 1968

Here we are, sitting out here in the bush on New Year's Day. I wonder what Charlie thought about our New Year's Eve celebration several hours ago. He might have been part of it since I did see some white and green tracers. By the way, we all shoot tracer rounds so we can tell where we are shooting when it's dark. They have white and green, and we have red. Anyhow, everybody started shooting anything and everything at midnight. There were flares, all kinds of bullets, artillery rounds that burst in the air, and generally one of the greatest fireworks shows I have ever seen. I'm surprised nobody got injured. That wasn't very peaceful for a peacekeeping truce, and these truces do not mean that gunfire isn't exchanged between us and them. That's been happening daily.

We had a dignitary visitor come out to our location today. Apparently, he is a congressional representative from the state of Texas. I know I'll be able to remember his name since Grandpa always called me George (not sure why, but it has something to do with lying or not lying), and of course, we are out in the bush. While he is riding around in one of those PACVs, I think I'll write a letter home.

Jan 1, 1968 – A Letter to Home

Dear Family,

Hi ya. Remember when I wrote last year on Christmas Day and told you we were out on an operation? Guess what? We still are. We got to go in for one day on December 27th for Christmas dinner, but early Thursday morning, we were on our way again. We're scheduled to go back tomorrow. This boat is getting pretty well-known. On the first day of our first mission the day before Christmas, we were credited for killing 14 VC. I don't guess that is anything to brag about, but we're still proud of it.

Not much has been happening the last few days, but the VC are all around us. I am looking forward to getting back to pick up my mail. I'm hoping for quite a bit. Got a Christmas card from Sandy L and Larry B on Christmas Day and a letter from Debbie N, too. Received your letter, John. The Navy brought mail to us last Friday or Saturday, I can't remember which. Every day is the same, you know.

Somebody (the Army or Navy) just brought in a hot meal for everybody. I don't know how they'll get it all served out. This being out in the middle of nowhere is getting me behind on my letter writing, but that's the way it goes. Tell Mrs. S at Palm thank you for the Christmas card, but don't tell her I don't know who she is. Say, Dad, if you want you can put my address in the Rotary paper. I enjoy receiving mail, and that's one way of getting my address around so people who like to write can. I hoped you put me in Palm's newsletter. Also, I hope I'm on Palm's mailing list.

If anybody wants to get me a present, a subscription to *Reader's Digest* would be nice.

You should see me. I haven't got my hair cut since the last time I was home, and it is plenty long and bushy. I have a beard and mustache. I am fairly dirty, haven't worn shoes in more than two weeks, have a pretty good tan now, wear ragged clothes, and otherwise look pretty much the same as last time you saw me. Only I'm fatter now. I know for a fact I weigh more than 150 pounds. That's all I got to say. Bye for now, and write soon.

Love,
Tom

Jan 5, 1968 – A Fifth of . . .

January—a new year and a new event. A few days ago, after getting back from our New Year's truce, there was a MEDCAP. A MEDCAP is a MEDical Civic Action Program operation. Various doctors go out with the boats to a village and provide medical services for the citizens. On the third, a bunch of reporters came out to see that ugly PACV. I seriously doubt they will decide to come out again since the PACV was shot at by the VC. Yesterday, a senator showed up, and this time I can easily remember his name. He's related to our previous president, John F. Kennedy. It's kind of fun to watch the faces of visitors as they see our lifestyle and environment.

It was not fun to do what we had to do today. About sunrise, we took off to try to locate a downed airplane. We did find it and had to provide security for it as the bodies and aircraft were recovered. Maybe tomorrow will be a better day. A bottle of booze would help.

Jan 6, 1968 – Mail Call

Dear Family,

Hi ya. Well today will be a slow day for once. We got back from an operation yesterday and will be going out again early tomorrow morning, but our boat is all ready to go, so it will give the crew a little free time.

We got paid Tuesday when we were in for the day. Was paid 141 dollars, but only drew 20. I want to save my money, you know. I have a plan. If you would, could you open a savings account in somebody's name of ya'll so you can draw money when I want you to? Come to think of it, although I have no money in the savings account I opened at Sterling's, I wonder if it still isn't good. Father, could you check with Mrs. V and see? And if it is good, send me some deposit slips and a booklet so I can send money to it. Or if it isn't good, open an account, and I will send you money orders to be put into it. I don't like the idea of leaving money on the books because the Navy has a bad habit of messing things up.

When I got paid, there was also a lot of mail for me that day. It sure made me feel good. I need to do a lot of writing today. Say, if you ever send me a package, could you include some writing materials like paper, pens, and envelopes? I never seem to have a chance to get them around here. Also, a couple bars of soap and maybe some cheap washcloths would be nice. It isn't that they aren't available, but there isn't the time when the store's open.

I can't think of much more to write about, so I guess I'll quit for right now.

Love,
Tom

Jan 8, 1968 – Gomer

Gomer. I have to explain my attitude and feelings about him. He knows how to play cards. He regularly wins and takes advantage of everybody and everything. He swaps and deals for stuff and fixes engines and other mechanical things. I just haven't liked being around him. He's the ultimate example of rude, crude, and an overall bad attitude. He is loud and obnoxious, dirty, slimy, and generally grimy. He barges in and tries to take charge of anything and everything that's around him. He is the Grinch and the Scrooge of a Christmas attitude, and he thinks he is the meanest, baddest, fun-loving dude. His exploits are outrageous, and his language is full of expletives. He doesn't care about others, love, or what's proper and right. He only cares about himself and what is in his sight.

Jan 9, 1968 – The Fight

Today is the 9th of January, and we are having a stand-down day. Got back from an operation yesterday (we were out for about two days on that one), and we are currently sitting in the well deck of Tango 91-4 having a casual conversation while we drink our two authorized and provided warm beers. Roger-Dodger, Robert, Frank, and I are talking about how cool the Air Force bombing strike alongside us was, how the Army found 5,000 bungee sticks, and how our boat division detained 77 suspected VCs all on the 7th. We talked about the excitement of yesterday when two VCs lost their lives trying to plant a water mine in front of our boats as we were landing troops. I guess those two won't try that again. One of the guys mentioned that apparently the Marine Corps Commandant paid a visit yesterday. Wonder what he thought about that incident.

Then Gomer shows up. We all know what he's been doing—scamming, trading, and harassing others so he can exceed his allotment of two warm beers. His actions and stagger show that he has been quite successful. The four of us are quite disgusted with his behavior. Although I am 19 years of age, I have never confronted anyone verbally much less physically. I chose to make a comment about him needing to go somewhere else. Some decisions bite back.

Gomer said, "Stand up and say that to my face." So I start to stand to repeat my comment. Whoops! Well, Gomer throws a punch that knocks me to the deck of the well deck. I'm not a fighter, but I am not a person who would back down from a fight that has been brewing and stewing. We go at it, punching, slugging, grabbing, choking, hitting, and slapping. Then we do it again, several times, again and again. No one is trying to break up this fight even while arms and legs are flying and flailing. I'm very conscious that no one else is getting involved. An inexperienced fighter and a drunken fighter must be a rather unusual sight for anyone. Someone starts to laugh, and within moments, all five of us are laughing so hard that the fight is insignificant. Someone makes a pungent statement: "Why are we trying to kill each other when we have an enemy out there trying to kill us?"

Jan 10, 1968 – The Home Front

We are out on another operation near Snoopy's Nose. The Army has been involved in a rather substantial battle for several hours. The last report said approximately 10 Army soldiers have lost their lives, and another 32 have been wounded. A couple of VC tried again to put mines in front of our landing craft as we were beaching our troops. This time, they were captured and lived. I think I'll write a letter home but not mention anything about this operation. It would probably upset the home front. The home front is now going back to our home on Sebastian instead of that newer home by Rubidoux High School. The new one is nice, but the old one is way better.

Dear Family,

Hi. What wonderful news to hear about the move. I can't wait to get back to that house. I might even live at home for the rest of my life. Thank you for the Macgregors' newsletter. And John, thanks ever so much for the *Readers Digest* subscription. The whole crew is happy about that. I have enclosed an article on a car I'm most interested in buying. If the Toyota dealer has any more information on it, I would greatly appreciate having it.

If you ever get around to sending me a package, be sure to include some instant iced tea with lemon already added. Some pocketbooks would be nice, too.

Palm Church is sending the weekly paper, and other mail is coming in pretty often. I can't really tell yet how long it takes for a letter to arrive because we're out on operations so much. But I think it takes about five days. Say, remember the girls I met the weekend of the reunion at Nadine's? One of them has been writing quite a bit. She's pretty nice. I can't think of much more to say, so I'll close. Bye for now.

Love,
Tom

Jan 15, 1968 – What's That?

Now I know we have been busy for days and days and days. I know that exhaustion can cause hallucinations. But I'm not that tired, and I know I don't know what that is. The official records say that UDT is testing a piece of equipment, but I know those guys are Navy SEALs. UDT and Navy SEALs are closely related, but at the same time, they are extremely different. I am not sure whether anyone in the States really knows that. The Frogmen with green faces have this new item. I just saw it today. I'm not sure how to describe it. If you could stand on it or sit on it, it would be a fantastic personal watercraft. And what a great piece of equipment it could be! It could be used as a water rescue tool or an extreme fun-producing, pleasurable water toy. They call it an Aqua DART, or Aquadart, and it's known as a swimmer assist vehicle. It has a fiberglass body and is about eight feet long. Probably weighs about 200 pounds and is very fast. The operator lies prone on the craft to present a minimum profile. Time will tell whether this goes well, but I'm here to say it would be fun to play with that water machine.

Jan 22, 1967 – A Letter to Home
(whoops, wrote that wrong – '68)

Dear Folks,

Got your package last Saturday night when I got back from an operation. Thank you. I've already used half of the iced tea, and the marshmallows were gone by noon yesterday, and the bag wasn't opened until after 11:00 a.m. The soap I needed, and I can use everything else. But may I make one request? Kool-Aid is fine, but it seems there is an overabundance of it going around, and at this moment, we have about 500 packages aboard our boat.

We had a few exciting moments this past week. We were involved in a firefight, but no boat took any hits, and only one man got wounded from shrapnel. I haven't had the time to write anybody for a week, so I am way behind.

I received the savings account thing. Will be taking care of that. Also, I received my first *Reader's Digest* yesterday but haven't started reading it yet. Hope to start today. We're going out again tonight or tomorrow on another operation. River Division 91, there are four divisions—91, 92, 111, and 112—that have been frontline company for two months now. We're only supposed to be it for a month, but we're so good they won't give us a rest. I've had a total of four hours of liberty since arriving here. I remember when I used to get 16 hours a day.

I filled out my dream sheet yesterday. I requested radioman school. I hope I get it. That would be about 20 weeks in San Diego.

Say hi to everybody for me. At the moment, I can't think of much more to write, and the boat is getting ready to leave for a new home next to an LST ship. So bye for now.

Love,
Tom

Jan 23, 1968 – The Catcher Reflector

I am sitting quietly in the middle of the boat in the middle of the night in the middle of nowhere reflecting about being in the middle of decisions I've made. I have chosen to join the military in a way that is against what my parents wanted for me. I said goodbye, don't want you in my life to one nice young lady, and have pursued another one who doesn't seem to want me in her life. I think we have already lost a crew member because I don't remember his name. I think about books I have read like *The Yearling* and *The Red Badge of Courage* and know they have something to do with me. I remember sneaking around and reading another book about some type of misfit, and I don't remember the book's name. Yes, I do. It was *The Catcher in the Rye*. How do you fit in when you don't fit in to what you think others want you to be? I know why I have chosen to be in this location and these circumstances, but I also know I cannot expect others to support it, nor should they be expected to deal with the repercussions of my decision. I cannot and will not endanger the lives of my shipmates, so I guess I will do the best I can, no matter what. It feels like a bad dream.

Life Can Be a Dream
  Life can be a dream,
  A nightmare or heaven supreme.
  Most of the time
  We live our dream
  In between.
  We are here as a team,
  There is no scheme
  That can delete our dream
  As we all scream
  "Make us free"
  From our dream!
  Do you know what that can mean
  To someone who's seen
  The reality of a bad dream?

Jan 24, 1968 – A Letter to Home

Dear Folks,

I have a few free moments, so I thought I'd write. I have another request to make. Could you send me all the information you can get on the Spitfire soft top Mark III? I can get it with quite a few extras for $2,100 tax free, stateside delivery.

We're supposed to go out on an operation tonight. Nothing much has been happening for the past few days. I need to write about 5,000 letters. My weight is still about 150, most of it in the belly. I'd write more, but we just got word it's time to go out on an operation for a few days. Bye.

Love,
Tom

Jan 25, 1968 – Bird of Paradise

We just finished one of those "little" firefights with a bunch of VCs shooting sporadic small arms at the boats while we were beached. Our ramps were lowered to the ground so we could retrieve returning Army soldiers who were also in a small arms firefight. It was one time we were not allowed to return fire since there were infantry guys out in front of us, and of course, most of our weapons are mounted on the boat to shoot to our sides. Our location was a little ironic since we were parked at a graveyard site. From the cox'n flat, it was easy to see a carved wooden bird that was on top of a grave marker. Well, Gomer could see the wooden bird from the well deck, and he wanted it. No one has ever claimed that Gomer uses wisdom to make his decisions. He tends to be rather spontaneous with his actions. He dashes from the relative safety in the well deck and sprints with a zigzag movement toward the grave marker and the wooden bird. The rate of the VC small arms fire suddenly increases and seems to be primarily directed at him. Somehow, he wrestles the bird away from its eternal perch and returns in his same running style to our boat. He survives in one piece, and so does the carving. He then presents it to the boat crew to be placed up at the cox'n flat as our good luck charm. We are so proud of him and it, and then we ask him to choose a name for our mascot. He responds, "Since we're living in a tropical wonderland, I'll name it Bird of Paradise."

I didn't know I would come to Vietnam to get the bird. Here is its rear end.

Jan 26, 1968 – A Letter to Home

Dear Folks,

Just a short note to say thanks for the wonderful package. Received it last night when we got back from an operation. The Levi's fit fine. And the writing material should last at least a week. The crew loves the marshmallows in their hot cocoa. The washcloth should help me keep clean. I plan on writing Jim L today or tomorrow or as soon as I can. The tea is delicious but not as good as a glass of homemade tea would be. I'm about the same as before, still fit and healthy. That's all for now.

Love,
Tom

Green Levi's and a JC Penney's pocket T, dress uniform of the day

Jan 28, 1968 – The Easy Day

I have heard the Navy SEALs have a saying: "The only easy day was yesterday." It has its own meaning.

If tomorrow is going to be hard compared to this day,
Why would anyone want to go that way?
"Each day has enough trouble of its own"
Is what one knows the Bible does say.
Don't think about self or go it alone.

I think I know or have heard about a book or a movie called something like *All Quiet on the Western Front.* It, like the other titles previously mentioned, has to do with what we are experiencing. The enemy has been quiet and hard to find and has asked for a 36-hour truce to celebrate their Lunar New Year. Tomorrow, we head for the infamous Snoopy's Nose to assume blocking positions of enemy movement. So is it our job to block them from having a time of enjoyment or to block their time of involvement? Only time will tell, and time *will* tell of a time in hell.

Jan 29, 1968 – Cigs and C-Rats

We are no longer the FNGs (new guys), and there are primarily two reasons. A new batch of sailors arrived from Mare Island to replace some of the original boat crews like we did. They are members of the class who started training after we did. That is one reason, and there is another. We have been in enough firefights to have lost our original virginity. I am starting to lose track of how many firefights have occurred. Part of losing track is how to decide if a firefight has even happened. Certainly, a sniper firing one shot is not a firefight, but I'm not sure how to consider several snipers firing several rounds each and our returning fire with everything we've got. I am sure those VC think they have been in a firefight, so maybe we have, too. After many of the firefights, we gathered as a crew to brew and drink a cup of instant coffee that we get from C-rat—combat rations—meals. We also like to enjoy a cigarette that comes from the meal packets.

There are 12 meals in each case of C-rats. Some of our rations are so old they have dates going back to the Korean War. Each meal comes in a box with several cans of food, and there is a little packet that has a spoon, napkin, toilet paper, chewing gum, and a packet of four cigarettes. As a boat crew, we also get packages from the Red Cross that include a carton of cigarettes. We don't need to buy cigarettes because of how many we can generate from C-rats and Red Cross packages. When we came aboard Tango 91–4, three cases of C-rats would easily last a whole day for our food supply. Now, we are using at least two cases per meal, and some of the crew who have been here for a while use a case per man per meal. I'm sure in time we will be the same way.

While enjoying our smokes and C-4 brewed coffee, we started a rather unusual activity. It is sort of based on the water survival swimming we learned at Mare Island. None of us like the idea of not being able to get the enjoyment of a cigarette. What happens if you lose a hand and there is no one around to help with getting a cigarette out of a pack and getting it lit? So we practice pulling a fresh unopened pack and a book of matches from any given pocket and getting a cigarette lit with only the left or the right hand. We are starting to get pretty good at doing it and can even compete against each other. There must be a better way to make a living.

Feb 8, 1968 – Ben Tre

We have been busy—too busy. I can't find that letter I wrote a couple days ago. General Westmoreland, the US commander in Vietnam, has stated that "the Mobile Riverine Force saved the Delta." He has written and is submitting a recommendation for the MRF to be given a Presidential Unit Award because:

> Throughout the Tet (Lunar New Year) Offensive, the Mobile Riverine Force (MRF) was locked in nearly continuous combat as the enemy lay siege to or threatened to attack every large population center and military installation in the Delta. In every battle, MRF personnel, both individually and collectively, although often matched against forces of much greater size than their own, displayed outstanding courage and professionalism in subduing the Viet Cong challenge. Navy crewmen embarked in Monitors, Command and Communication Boats, Assault Support Patrol Boats, and Armored Troop Carriers. They were frequently ambushed at point-blank range from concealed positions along both banks of the narrow, jungle-enshrouded Delta streams. In each instance, they succeeded in suppressing the enemy fire before maneuvering their assault craft out of ambush areas. Together, the MRF Army-Navy team successfully met the challenge posed by the Tet Offensive, probably saving the Delta from being overrun by insurgent forces.

Ben Tre, one of the locations General Westmoreland knows we saved, is a big village or a small town very close to the Crossroads, and we love the kids in the area. Ben Tre is more famous than most realize. In 1959, a female Viet Cong general, Nguyen Thi Dinh, led guerrillas in an uprising against the US-backed Saigon regime. Some say this was the real start of the Vietnam War. Graham Greene, a famous author and connoisseur of trouble spots, was in Ben Tre in

1951, and on the way back from Ben Tre to Saigon, he conceived the idea for his novel *The Quiet American* about the fall of French colonialism raging in Vietnam.

Yesterday, correspondent Peter Arnett reported that a 9th Infantry Division Major said, "It became necessary to destroy the town (Ben Tre) in order to save it." I know there was fierce hand-to-hand fighting in Ben Tre's streets. American jets and artillery leveled most of the town, and our troops were inserted to prevent it from being completely overrun. More than half the homes were destroyed. The death toll was so great that after a few days, both Viet Cong and South Vietnamese troops stopped fighting briefly. To prevent an epidemic, they disposed of dead soldiers and civilians in the river. Dead bodies in the river— that is the water we live in and on.

This whole situation makes me think about a song that came out several years ago called "Mr. Custer." It is a song that is sung by a young man who is with the 7th Calvary as they are about to be attacked. With trembling in his voice, he says common phrases such as "What am I doing here?" and "I don't want to go" and "Please don't make me go." He dreams about the coming fight when someone yells "attack," and he stands there with an arrow in his back.

Where is that letter I wrote?

Feb 10, 1968 – Misplaced Letter

A few days ago, when we tied up alongside our ships for a few hours to resupply and refresh ourselves, I managed to write a short letter home. It is amazing that after eight days of bloodied combat it was so easy to be nonchalant when writing home. Temporarily losing the letter disturbed me more than the ordeals we had just participated in. I wonder what those at home are hearing about this thing called Tet. Now that I have found the letter, I need to get it sent home.

05 Feb '68

Dear Folks,

Howdy! Well I just got paid, so you'll find plenty of money in this envelope. Spend it wisely. Of course, the wisest way would be to put it in the savings account. Next month's pay I will keep for R&R. And the next month, too. Also, I plan on joining the Navy Credit Union. At first, I will be saving money through them, and then I will borrow some to buy a car. Insurance for the car will be bought through the union, and payments will be combined. I will be allotting $100 a month to the union. When I buy my car, I will take a 36-month loan, and $50 a month will be for the car and $50 for savings. When I have enough in savings to pay off the balance of the loan, I will do so. Simple, isn't it? The Navy has a way for everything. Ha ha!

Enclosed you have found some pictures of me. Please don't burn them. As you can tell, I am a well-dressed sailor.

Well, that's all for this letter. Bye.

Love,
Tom

Feb 15, 1968 – This Tet Thing

For almost two weeks, the VC has been going crazy in the southern part of South Vietnam. The military newspaper *Stars and Stripes* reports that it's even been longer up in the northern part at a place called Hue and someplace called Khe Sanh. Glad I am not there. I have to tell the family something, so I'd better write home.

15 Feb '68

Dear Folks & John,

Hi ya. Just received a lot (and I mean mucho) of mail. It was almost completely cut off during the last two weeks because of the outbreak by the VC. But now it's all here, and once again, I'm way behind in my letter writing. Thanks for the packages. I got the one from the fifth-grade class and the one with nuts and the one with candy. Thanks again. I got a piece of mail mailed Jan 9th (I think) from John. It had some pretty funny pictures.

Boy! These past two weeks have been something else. We've had some pretty close calls, and the Viet Cong did manage to do some damage, but we hit them harder. The riverboats (not including the Army it carries) managed to kill more than 300 Viet Cong. And the Army killed many more, of course. The last letter I told of an ambush. Well, there was another. We weren't so lucky in it. When I say "we," I mean the whole river squadron, not the boat. The boat was one of the very few lucky ones. We didn't even receive a mark.

Say hi to everybody for me. By the way, I'm curious to know what furniture you have where. Seems to me the family room and living room could be bare.

Bye for now.

Love,
Tom

When I decided to come here, I didn't think about needing to write home. It would be much easier for me if I didn't, but I would not want them not knowing whether I am alive or not.

Feb 20, 1968 – Jacquie

It is the middle of the night, whatever that might mean. We are cruising around our Riverine ships on a patrol called BID. I have no idea what BID stands for, but I know what it means. It means we are delegated to do what we can do to protect the ships that provide our life support. We are required to throw all kinds of grenades such as concussion and fragment types into the water to kill anything around us or the ships. We can also shoot at (with anything we've got) moving objects in the water. Thanks to Gomer, we have quite a selection of guns beyond our normal armament. He has managed to wheel and deal (hopefully not steal) a 357 Magnum, a thing called a grease gun, a Tommy Gun (Thompson submachine gun), and an enemy's AK 47, and he doesn't care if we play with his toys. It does not take the whole crew to be in combat positions. Some can sleep (how with the noise?) while others do the chores. We have a crew of six, and three can do the duties that are needed. To me, BID could stand for Bothered Internally by Decisions. It doesn't bother me about deciding to come to Vietnam. It doesn't bother me why I decided to come to Vietnam. It doesn't bother me to be away from home because of Vietnam. I don't care that today is Valentine's Day, but I am bothered by my decision to reject Jacquie. Am I at a crossroads? I need to make a decision.

Feb 21, 1968 – Dear Jacquie

Dear Jacquie,

I have heard that you are going to college in Arkansas. I hope that is going good for you. When we last saw each other, I was not very kind and said some things I should not have. If you want to ignore this letter, that would be all right, and I wouldn't blame you. I do want you to know that I miss having you as part of my life. I don't know whether I will get through this year, but if I do, I hope we can still be friends. We have had some good times and, I guess, a few that weren't so good. Roy was a little upset with us at the all-night grad party at Disneyland. I did enjoy your visits to that little apartment in San Diego. You missed a good going away party. I learned that I enjoy a good cold beer, but the beer we have here is not good or cold.

I want you to know that you are important to me and that I think of you often. Tell your mom and dad hi for me, and I will write again if you want.

Yours truly,
Tom

Feb 25, 1968 – Looking at Self and Others

There are those who say
I'm going the wrong way.
How can they know that
When I don't know where I'm at?
I know I'm in the Nam
But where did I come from?
You live for a dream
And die with a scream.
How do they know what I mean?
I'm here for a chosen scheme.
But just what does that mean?
I look around and see
That no one's looking at me.
They are looking at themselves,
Maybe putting me on a shelf.
I'll get off this shelf and test
And then try to find what is best
For others to look around and see
What He wants them to be.

Rodger-Dodger looks for a reprieve,
He's wanting a break from this misery.
He needs a trip to see his lady
Because she's going to have a baby.
Gomer is being Gomer as no one else can be.
He's just a man looking to live so very free.
Frank has been taking many a picture
And trying to see what's in the future.
Robert's view on the life ahead
Doesn't give sight to any dread.

Feb 27, 1968 – Love

I have come to believe that one of the toughest things in life is dealing with the middle of the night. Whether you're cruising around the Tastee-Freez in Rubidoux or cruising around on ships in the South China Sea, the darkness encircles you, and you get this feeling, "What am I doing here?" Like the song about Gen. Custer, you think, "I don't want to go," but just what do I, or anyone else, really know? What do I know about love? What is love? Is love painfully hung up on a pretty girl with a ponytail? Or with one that I know so well? What do I love? The thought of being alive or the thought about not being here—whether it is life or death. Around and around and around I go, and where I stop, nobody knows. But this I know—what I don't know—why do I love when I don't know what love is? What do you get from love? What are the choices of love? What are the definitions of love that haven't been explained? God is love, and God is light. But this darkness of night hides what I want to find is right. Who or what do I love? And what are the choices in the middle of the night?

Feb 28, 1968 – Not Much News

Dear Folks & John,

Hi ya. I think it's been a while since I last wrote. Sorry about that. Received a sweet tooth package. Thanks. It was yummy. Say, John, I received a couple of nice letters from Bobbie. Jacquie wrote and told me to tell you hi from Ark. Not much news to tell you. Oh yeah, I got the soap box and have already put it to use. I cleaned my rack (bed). I hate to tell you this, but this is a short letter.

Love always,
Tom

"Not much news to tell you." I guess that hides the fact that we've been on an operation for almost 10 days with numerous firefights and even some fatalities, that 15 plank owners (original boat crew members) were wounded at Tan Son Nhat Airport in Saigon while they were trying to return home after their year tour, that Jacquie and I are writing each other and my thoughts are becoming more and more confused (tomorrow is Leap Year Day—that means the cute blonde has her fifth birthday celebration as she turns 20, and how can I think about her when I'm also thinking about Jacquie?).

Not Much News to Tell You
The thoughts are many, but the words are few
I need to return to the library, I'm long overdue.
The library is peaceful and a place of solitude
"Quiet please" is the basic attitude.
There's "not much news to tell you."

Mar 1, 1968 – A Day in the Life of . . .

Many of the people at home have been writing and asking what a day is like. Well, a day in the life of a Riverine sailor is basically like everyone else's in this world. We get up in the morning—wait, that may not be quite true. We frequently stay up all night when out on operations or patrol, and, of course, at least two of us have to be awake 24/7 to operate the boat if necessary and to make sure it's not sinking. We don't know when an operation will start or end until just a couple of hours before that happens, and operations may start at any time of the day based on who's going where and how long it will take to get there, and 2 a.m. is just as common as sunrise or later in the day. Many people take a shower first thing in the morning, but we only take showers if we happened, by chance, to be tied up alongside a ship with available free time, and that's not very often.

A lot of folks enjoy having breakfast first thing, and I guess we do, too; however, our breakfast may consist of a can of turkey loaf, some crackers, chocolate bar (disk), maybe a can of peaches, and some more crackers. Breakfast might be enjoyed while standing in a gun mount, standing at the helm, or maybe sitting on our butts down in the well deck if not much is going on. The well deck might not be available if there are 40 some-odd soldiers lounging in it.

Now, the first work order of the day is to make sure all weapons are ready to go, loaded, and a good resupply of ammunition and gun parts are available. That is more important than whether the boat can operate. You can't defend a broken boat with broken guns. After guns are taken care of, it's time to take care of the boat. There are repairs, maintenance, cleaning, and resupplying general needs, including and primarily medical supplies. You can't defend a broken boat with broken people. You've got to be able to patch them up.

Now, it's time for lunch. Lunch may consist of a can of turkey loaf, some crackers, chocolate bar (disk), maybe a can of peaches, and some more crackers. Lunch might be enjoyed while standing in a gun mount, standing at the helm, or maybe sitting on our butts down in the well deck if not much is going on. The well deck might not be available if there are 40 some-odd soldiers lounging in it.

After lunch and the above-needed work focuses, there may be time to take care of people—ourselves. There is laundry to be done, and the bucket we use is a toilet, and we use the water of the brown rivers. We don't do laundry very often because there is no one to impress with our clothing. We don't have or wear very much clothing anyhow. After laundry, maybe we take a river bath (same bucket).

After the guns, the boats, and the people have all been taken care of, it's probably time for dinner. Dinner may consist of a can of turkey loaf, some crackers, chocolate bar (disk), maybe a can of peaches, and some more crackers. Dinner might be enjoyed while standing in a gun mount, standing at the helm, or maybe sitting on our butts down in the well deck if not much is going on. The well deck might not be available if there are 40 some-odd soldiers lounging in it.

When nighttime rolls around, we basically try to stay alive and, as needed, stay awake to do what needs to be done when it needs to be done. All the above basically occurs even if we are on an operation, on patrol, or tied up next to a ship. It's just a day in the life.

During the night, we might have a snack of some kind. A snack may consist of a can of turkey loaf, some crackers, chocolate bar (disk), maybe a can of peaches, and some more crackers. A snack might be enjoyed while standing in a gun mount, standing at the helm, or maybe sitting on our butts down in the well deck if not much is going on. The well deck might not be available if there are 40 some-odd soldiers lounging in it. Such is life in a day of. . . .

PS: There might have been a firefight or two (or more) during the day, but that's another story.

Mar 6, 1968 – Bad Language

It has been a week since I last wrote the family, so I need to think seriously about doing that chore. I really do enjoy receiving mail, but at times it is so difficult to respond. There are certainly time limitations, location limitations, and my spelling and grammar limitations. It's good not to be at college trying to get through English classes. I would have to be scared of being kicked out and being sent to Vietnam. *Usin' sum badd langage arond hear ain't no big deel.* And there is plenty of bad language around here to hear.

06 Mar '68

Dear Family,

Hi ya. Have received a couple of packages from you lately. The nuts were good, and the iced tea took care of thirst after eating them. Got the box with the peanut brittle. It made my fingers sticky, but it was worth it. It had been a while since I had something sweet like that. I'm not in need of much except liberty, and there's nothing you could do about that. I could use a mail answering service. I don't think I'll buy a car until I get home. I want to test drive it first, and a car depends a lot on my orders. You never know when or where I might be going next. I've taken out a savings allotment, and I'll increase it after R&R. Right now, it's $50, but around June I'll raise it to $150. I'll still send some money home but not much. Maybe $10 a month, but that won't be until after R&R either.

I just now finished reading a letter from y'all (written Feb 25). Seems from what Kathy writes and what you tell me that marriage is the new fad in Riverside. I've been wondering where the boxes have been coming from. They always arrive in good condition.

One division of boats has taken a little trip. They're at the DMZ. I don't know what they're doing. Maybe I'm not supposed to. Our division is back on the front line. A boat division is supposed to be on a four-month rotation, but not us. We're so tough we get front line every other month. My division has had the least deaths in the first year of operation; there were only two. Did I ever tell you my boat is credited with 14 killed VC? That's all for today.

Love,
Tom

Well that letter only contained a few half-truths. I don't intend to buy the car I've been looking at previously, but I am seriously considering a new car that is to be produced by Nissan, that's Datsun in the US, and the two deaths were from the first of the year, not the whole previous past year.

Mar 12, 1968 – All Quiet on the Western Front

All Quiet on the Western Front, but we must be in Far East Asia and nowhere near any Western front unless it's a weather storm. As Erich Maria Remarque, the author of the novel, says, "This book is to be neither an accusation nor a confession, and least of all an adventure, for death is not an adventure to those who stand face to face with it." The book does not focus on heroic stories of bravery but rather gives a view of the conditions in which the soldiers find themselves. I cannot disagree with him when I consider what I am writing in this diary. There has been a death and several other casualties from what is called friendly fire. The gunships were doing what they had to do in order to save the majority of lives. There have been numerous firefights over the last several days. One Army fellow lost his life from falling overboard, and he happened to be a brother of a Riverine sailor. There has been a memorial service for five Riverine sailors who recently lost their lives. "All Quiet on the Western Front," but we must be in Far East Asia and nowhere near any Western front unless it's the storm we are weathering.

Mar 14, 1968 – All Noise in the Far East

Tango boats are heavier than tanks. Lifting anything out of the water scientifically will seem even heavier than it is. An estimated 500-pound mine was placed in the Cua Viet River at the DMZ. A Tango boat, T-112-7 found it the hard way. While minesweeping on the river from a little outpost called Cua Viet and going to a little village called Dong Ha, the boat was not only lifted up and out of the water, but it was flipped. The boat was destroyed, but worse, so were the lives of six of the seven-man crew. This loss is especially significant because I believe the crew was a crew I trained with back in the States. It is bad down here in the Delta. I just hope I never have to go to Cua Viet.

"Meanwhile, back at the ranch" (Delta), an Alpha boat was also destroyed by a mine, but the crew survived. If I don't write home soon, I won't survive when I do get home, so here goes.

14 Mar '68

Dear Folks & John,

Hi ya! From what I understand, the mailman has been having trouble. I have been writing, but you haven't been receiving. I must admit I haven't been writing a lot lately, but not to the point where you shouldn't have received any letters for three weeks. Maybe the mail service will improve, I doubt it. I got the package from the fifth grade class today. Chewed most of the gum in one day. We're like that here. We chew for flavor only. More and more people are writing all the time, and it's hard to keep up. Very hard. But I try.

One of the crew members on the boat has a father working in Vietnam, and last night they got to see each other for the first time in two years. Right now, they're playing poker with two other crew members.

About the tennis shoes. I will be needing another pair in about two months. That way I can use them for R&R when new. Anytime you want to send another box of soap and bleach will be fine. No hurry. What would be nice is canned food like chili, tamales, peaches, orange juice, etc. I have candy (sweets), but it tends to get sticky because of heat and dampness. Kind of messy, but still good to eat.

Well, that's all for today.

Love,
Tom

Apr 4, 1968 – 47 Nicks and Gouges

I do not personally remember December 7, 1941, known as "the day of infamy, but I will always remember April 4, 1968 as a day of infamy. The ships of the Riverine Force have spent many days anchored in the river between My Tho and Dong Tam. During those days of anchorage, the ships received numerous rocket and mortar attacks from the south. A huge operation was designed to infiltrate the area of the south bank of the river by coming in from a more southern small stream loaded with troops and ready for war. Some RivDiv 91 boats have been chopped to work with River Division 92 for a cruise to the Crossroads and up Ambush Alley.

As we approach our initial landing site, a firefight breaks out between the VC and us. We proceed farther than the landing site and turn our boats for the beach. As we get near the beach, another firefight erupts. We reverse our boats, re-form, and proceed farther west. We have had numerous two-site ambushes but never one with a third entrenchment. A few days ago, we did experience three firefights in one afternoon, but they were at completely different locations and a couple hours apart each time. Once again, we turn our boats for the shore, hit the embankment, and start lowering our ramps so the Army can charge off and flank the enemy ambush sites.

Then it happens! As the ramps hit the ground, the boat to our left receives an RPG round into the well deck. As Tango 4's ramp hits the ground, a 51-caliber machine gun opens up and starts shooting into our well deck. All the boats are receiving heavy rocket and automatic weapon fire. The boats are ordered to retract from the shoreline, and as we do so, numerous soldiers are trying to return to the boats and are in the water with enemy weapons aimed and firing at them. Utter chaos ensues. Andy, we call him Ollie, Twist climbs out of the well deck of Tango 3 and starts pulling people out of the water and throws them onto his boat. Tracer rounds are flying all around him. I have never witnessed a braver man. That's worth repeating. "I have never witnessed a braver man."

The boats limp back to the Crossroads where the boats are reorganized, and the available Army personnel are also regrouped. The revamped but smaller force then proceeds back to the area of contact but are unable to return fire at the enemy because of the troops stuck in the foliage along the sides of the stream. (About two weeks ago, the military started spraying the banks in order to eliminate the ability of the enemy to fortify and hide themselves in the foliage.) Battle damage assessment: Numerous boats damaged and temporarily disabled; 22 US KIAs; 120 US WIAs; the three Navy KIAs were all in their boat's cox'n flats.

A boat cox'n flat has two sides and the front with fold-up steel plates that measure approximately 2 feet by 3 feet by 1 inch. Each plate has slits that can be used as viewing ports. The side steel flaps have a sliding portion that is kind of like a window that measures about 1 foot by 1 foot. Up until the morning of the 4th, I have always kept my little sliding window open so I could see the exterior world better. For some reason (God's providence), it was closed. As the evening approached, I looked at the outside surface of my little window where my head had been during the battle. I counted 47 nicks and gouges from enemy weapons that ricocheted off my window to the world.

Battle damage to a sliding window

Apr 7, 1968 – Gomer, the Miracle Worker

The boat crew is waiting for the repair ship mechanics to finish fixing one of the boat's engines. We have been on idle time since yesterday evening when we arrived at the floating repair facilities. It is personally gut-wrenching to explain the whys and hows of this insignificant adventure.

There was a disastrous big battle on April 4th. Late morning on the 5th, we received a rather unusual order. Tango 91-4 was given an assignment to head upstream through Ambush Alley. We were given map coordinates of our destination and then given instructions to stay in that immediate vicinity and just float, cruise, idle, and linger. In other words, we were being sent out to be a viable target for Charlie to shoot at. The big game plan included an all-out attack by troop loaded helicopters, gunships, artillery, and a river convoy of assault rivercraft. They would come to our rescue and relieve Charlie of his life-flowing blood.

As we headed to our assigned deathtrap, we all lit up our handy C-rats allotment of cigarettes. We each held a lit cigarette for about two and a half hours. One match was all that was ever needed to keep us puffing. Around half of a carton was consumed. The fear of the unknown can be excruciating. We didn't know what would be used to shoot at us or what damage it might do if, in spite of their poor accuracy, they managed to strike their target—us.

We survived that escapade, and yesterday morning, the 6th, we were informed that we would once again be used as a floating target. The crew climbed and gathered at the top of the boat by the cox'n flat and the three gun mounts. We sat or stood looking at each other but saying nothing. No one knew what to say or how to say anything. Suddenly, Gomer walked away and went to the interior of the boat. He returned in a little while and reported to the boat captain that one of the two engines was malfunctioning. He briefly explained that the malfunction would take many hours to fix, and tools that he did not have would be needed. The boat captain left to make a report to the river division commander. When he returned, he said we had been ordered to return to our mobile base and get the needed repairs. We tucked our tails between our legs, lowered our heads, and shamefully rode in silence to our reprieve. All the operation force returned, and we were told the deathtrap game plan was scratched.

Apr 11, 1968 – Decisions, Decisions, Decisions

I know I am approaching a crossroad in any emotion, thought, or plan.

Got to take a look at life and then take a stand.

When I'm awake, it is easy to think about Jacquie.

Though some might think I might be a little bit wacky.

I left Jackie in a most disturbing way,

but I have to admit, I now think of her every single day.

But when I'm sleeping, and even though that's not often,

I dream about another one who is so very far away.

Like Jacquie, she has been the dream of my life since about sixth grade.

I know that's not so long ago, and I know I'm not very old,

But this experience is taking a toll, and I need to decide who is one I can hold.

The dream girl has been friendly and kind, and she is on my mind,

But it is Jacquie, Jacquie, who I want to find.

If I can make it through this year, and I am still not sure whether I want to, a decision must be made in spite of fear about the one that's to be the focus of my dreams in real life, the one I want to be my wife.

Apr 14, 1968 – Twists and Turns

Two years ago, it was getting close to graduation time at Rubidoux High School. Neil Diamond came out with his new song, "Solitary Man," and I immediately attached it to the blonde girl of my dreams. At the all-night graduation party at Disneyland, the group known as The Association played a new song called "Cherish." I immediately attached it to the one I was sitting with, Jacquie, but she had come with a fellow classmate, Roy. I had invited somebody else to the event, but she was now with my buddy Paul. Life is just full of twists and turns, just like the muddy brown waters of the Mekong Delta. It can be a daily occurrence to twist and turn each of those songs to either one of those sweethearts. I have to wonder, will this be a lifelong occurrence?

Twisting and turning occurred this evening to the detriment of my being. We were sitting on the boat exchanging smokes and wondering what life was like for the folks we had left at home. While smoking and joking, I took a toke of my cigarette and flipped it to the air, wondering, "It will land where?" Pressed between my thumb and my middle finger, it was not meant to linger but fly up and away when flipped. It made its trip up so far away and then twisted and turned and started coming my way. Everyone was spellbound by its trip through the atmosphere, and my heart was pounding for a moment from fear as the cigarette made its final twist and turn and flew into my nose. "Blowin' smoke" is not a phrase to take lightly when a cigarette lands in your nostril and burns away. As the "Mr. Custer" song says, "Hey charlie, duck yer head! Hm, you're a little bit late on that one, charlie. Ooh, I bet that smarts!"

Wanting to attach to a female is like Peter, Paul, and Mary's version of "Blowin' in the Wind." Is there an answer? You twist and turn and try to begin to make decisions so someone can win. You win some, you lose some, but oh my, my, my, you are so lonesome.

Apr 17, 1968 – Light My Fire

Before I broke up with Jacquie, The Doors came out with a song called "Light My Fire." Jacquie did not understand, but I like that song so much, even at my young age. I've attached many songs to the gals of my life, and even though I'm still not quite yet a man, I can take that song and understand there is something about "light my fire." You take a match, strike it on a flint, and I'll give you a hint about your circumstances beyond your control. You have to wonder, when is your final hour? No one said life would be easy or that it would be fun. I'm just trying to figure out when my life has begun. I don't know whether I'm starting to live or I'm looking at death in the face. I have already seen many lives that can't be replaced. This task I've chosen is a burden right now. I don't know whether I want to live or die, but there is one thing I can tell, I don't want to send anyone to hell.

Recently, I got into trouble for not writing home, so I think I will elaborate on what I did send.

17 Apr '68

Dear Folks,

Well, I know it's been a few days since I last wrote, but "ol' Charlie" keeps us running, or should I say he keeps running, and we have to stay on his tail. We averaged more than 300 hours a month out on operations, plus all the time spent repairing, maintaining, and resupplying our boat. That's a full-time job, and it has to be done during the day, or do it in the dark because we're not allowed to use white lights after sundown. At night, the only thing there is to do when there's nothing to do (?) is listen to the radio, talk, and sleep. We do a lot of all three. There are a few TVs around, but they're small, and the crowds are so large that it's not worth it to watch it. Thanks for all the iced tea. It came just in time. My R&R will be sometime in late May or June at either Australia or Singapore. That's all I know. Easter Sunday was spent out in the field just like Christmas, New Year's, and every other holiday. We haven't missed one yet.

Well, that's all for now.

Love,
Tom

Apr 24, 1968 – Love Is Blue

Roger-Dodger went back to the "real world" last month for about a week for the birth of his baby boy. When he came back, he just kept talking and talking and talking, and maybe even talking some more about some kind of beautiful song that was the current number-one hit. It had something to do with love being blue. Every chance we get to hear the military radio station (AFRS), we hope to hear it, and we finally have. I have to admit that the instrumental by Paul Mauriat is absolutely beautiful. I have attached songs to others, but there has always been one song I attach to all, and that's the one by the Lettermen called "When I Fall in Love." The station even followed the presentation with a version that included words, and now I'm in a quandary. Do I love the thought of death or the thought of life? Do I love someone who is willing to share our life? Do I love life enough to make someone my wife? I have, and I bet I always will dwell on that Lettermen's song. It started somewhere around the seventh grade, and since I don't know what love is now, how could I have known what it was way back then? This I do know:

> Blue, blue, my love is blue.
> If I only knew
> Which to choose.
> Loving two doesn't change the hue
> Of the colors in my mind
> Or trying to find
> A way to start life anew.

May 1, 1968 – Darkness and Light

Well, we have left a combat zone, that wonderful place known as Ambush Alley and the Crossroads. You know, several weeks ago, I think six or seven, we had three firefights in one day. And then about four weeks ago, we had a triple ambush in one place. But now, yesterday, we surpassed all the previous times that surpassed all the previous times. We were back at Ambush Alley territory, and we all knew we could expect a good (?) and rowdy time. But this time was beyond being rowdy. The daily summary report of yesterday will record there was a total of seven firefights, and it will also record that River Division 91 accounted for five of those firefights. It's not always good to be the winner in accumulated numbers. The accumulation of death and wounded takes its toll on those who survive. To be a survivor means to survive, and then you go on and on a little bit more, but what do you do when you feel like more is more than enough? I guess you suck it up, count your losses, and press forward, but sometimes pressing forward might mean you're retreating into a deep, dark place. Being in a deep, dark place means you need some light in your world, and I have discovered that the children and the kids of Vietnam are a bright spot in my life. The kids have resilience in their lives that goes beyond the death and destruction that surrounds them. It is good to be surrounded by the bright youthfulness of life. Well, we're out of the combat zone (for now), that wonderful place known as Ambush Alley.

Vietnamese children

May 8, 1968 – Seeds

I have written about Charlie, my friend, when I started this journal. A few days ago, he fell overboard. Charlie was a superb athlete and the size of a typical professional football player. He was not a good swimmer and was somewhat scared of the water. When I walked off the boat this morning and stepped onto a pontoon, I almost stepped onto a body. The body was Charlie. He was now bigger from bloating, and his beautiful dark skin was now white from the decomposition of having been in the water so long.

If I was a farmer, I could look to the future and make a reasonable guess of what might be out there based on the seeds I have planted. Seeds will need nourishment, and seeds are the choices we make. If I don't know what seeds I have planted, I really won't know what to expect in the future since those choices are the seeds of tomorrow. I have to expect that I will have a tomorrow, but tomorrow never seems to come. As Shakespeare once wrote, "Tomorrow, and tomorrow, and tomorrow. Creeps in this petty pace from day to day. To the last syllable of recorded time," and today I need answers for the questions I will have tomorrow. Life is a stage "full of sound and fury," and the seeds planted have a theme of "signifying nothing." I only have time for answers for the seeds I have planted. My friend Charlie planted a seed of friendship when he caught that rabbit at Survival School. It was a seed that never really got nourished or had a chance to flourish. He planted his seed in a time for tomorrow that we did not yet know would be so full of sorrow. If I could look back so I could look forward and try to borrow some time from the past to plant seeds in furrows, maybe, just maybe, I could make seed choices that are not empty or hollow.

May 9, 1968 – Play It Again, Sam

We arrived back at our Mobile Riverine base today after an excursion similar to the one we had a month ago on April 4th. We were playing games again in the Crossroads (Ambush Alley) area and managed to be involved in two separate firefights yesterday afternoon when 14 Navy guys were wounded, and four boats received major damage. It was one of those firefights when so many rockets are fired that our boats catch them without detonating the explosives. The boats have heavy steel plating all around them, and that makes the boat so heavy that it would sink if it did not have big blocks of Styrofoam on the sides to help it float. The Styrofoam is held in place by something called bar armor. When a rocket hits between the bars, it can penetrate into the Styrofoam and not explode. It is a strange sensation to drive a boat with live, ready-to-explode RPGs dangling off its sides. You do what you have to do, and what I have to do is write Mom. Her birthday is coming up, and Sunday is Mother's Day.

09 May '68

Dear Mom,

Well, your birthday and Mother's Day are coming up soon, but I'm afraid there won't be any presents or even a card. It's not because I'm not thinking of you but because of present conditions around here. I want you to know that I am thinking of you daily. I know I don't write as often as you would like, but if you don't hear from me for a couple of weeks, don't be alarmed. It's just that we're busy, and time is passing faster than I realized. Also, there is a definite mail problem. I know of many lost letters that I have written.

I guess you know I'm changing, not so much in appearance or personality but in thinking. A person learns what he really likes or dislikes over here, and that statement brings to mind another line of thought that you should know about. I believe you know that I have been writing Jacquie. After being over here a few weeks, I found out just how much I really missed her. I didn't realize that I love her so much. I thought I could forget about her by going to another girl, but I was a fool.

I believe you can expect me home by Thanksgiving. So far, everybody is getting relieved a month early, so if luck holds out, it will be the same for me.

Well, it's time for me to go take a shower before supper. There's always plenty of hot water for showers, provided we're alongside the ship.

I want to wish you a very happy birthday and Mother's Day. Be sure to have Dad treat you to dinner for me. Have him take the money out of the savings account and then go to someplace nice, like the Ambassador in LA. Don't feel shy about using the savings money. There's plenty more where that came from, and besides, I can afford it. So have a good time, and write and tell me about it. And I'll check the savings account book when I get home, so I'd better find at least $20 missing, or I'll be hurt.

Love always.

Your son,
Tom

May 15, 1968 – Chasing the Wind

I had a disturbing occurrence last night. The Army lives aboard our Navy ships. The Navy boat crews might have a bunk or two available on the ship, but most of us, most of the time, lived 24/7 on the boats. There were reports of an Army guy going around and groping guys during the nighttime. I chose to "sleep" aboard the ship to see if I could be part of capturing this fellow. No formal plan was made by anyone on how, what, when, or whether anything was going to occur. As I lay on the bunk, I heard someone walking around. He came up to my rack, placed his hand on my crotch, and started to fondle me. I immediately yelled, but I don't remember what I yelled. He started running, and so did I, chasing him while other guys followed. We chased him up and out of the ship. We chased him across the pontoon where the boats were tied up. When he reached the end of the pontoon, he ran across some boats, and then he jumped or fell into the river. We ran to the edge of the boat and stopped. We stood there for a while, and then I went back to my boat. I have heard that an Army man has been listed as MIA.

My Wind-Blown Thoughts
Battered by the Holy Words of King Solomon in Ecclesiastes

I applied myself to search for understanding about everything in the universe. I discovered that the lot of man, which God has dealt to him, is not a happy one. It is all foolishness, chasing the wind. What is wrong cannot be righted; it is water over the dam, and there is no use thinking of what might have been.

I have thought deeply about all that goes on here in the world, where people have the power to injure each other. But though a man sins a hundred times and still he lives, I know very well that those who fear God will be better off, unlike the wicked who will not live long, good lives. Their days shall pass away as quickly as shadows because they don't fear God.

God's ways are as mysterious as the pathway of the wind and as the manner in which a human spirit is infused into the little body of a baby while it is yet in its mother's womb. Keep on sowing your seed, for you never know what will grow—and perhaps it all will.

Here is my final conclusion. Fear God, and obey His commandments, for this is the entire duty of humanity. For God will judge us for everything we do, including every hidden thing, good or bad.

May 20, 1968 – What Do You Really Mean?

May 20, '68

Dear Folks and John,

Howdy. Things are about the same (yeah, like another 14 guys got wounded a few days ago in a double firefight afternoon). On Mother's birthday, we made a big move (62 miles at 5 miles per hour and only one firefight). We're just outside Saigon right now (but still in the middle of nowhere with Viet Cong all around), but will be returning to Dong Tam in two days (yet we will still be out in the middle of the river, i.e., nowhere). We're extremely busy with operations, but every few days, we take a day off and relax (so we can reload with ammunition, C-rats, and other necessary supplies and do repair and maintenance on the boat, stand guard duty, launder our meager clothes, and so on). In eight days, it's time for my boat to go in the yards (but that's not a play yard; it's a work yard). Then it's time for R&R (R&R means rest and relaxation, but we consider it more to mean rowdy and rebellious), but I still don't know the place or dates. I'm ready anyhow (I am wondering if I'll still be an innocent boy when I return). Have received many greatly appreciated goodies like pudding, tamales, etc. Y'all are doing a wonderful job of keeping up my morale (Really? Then why is my morale so low?) and making life more comfortable (Really? How?). You'll never know how much it means because words aren't enough to say thanks (I really do mean that).

Say, have I ever told you about my souvenirs? They include one M2 carbine rifle that I will sell instead of bring home (unless I can figure out how to smuggle it home like some of the other guys are doing), the first flag my boat flew for the first year of operation, 140 slides and pictures, and I have only begun (but

I probably have finished since I am so jealous of Frank's 35 mm pictures), an old man's cigarette tobacco and paper kit, Viet money, and more that I haven't gotten yet. The *Riverside County Record* is coming now. It's great to read about home. Well, it's time for chow (more C-rats cooked over C4), so bye for now.

Love,
Tom

Jun 1, 1968 – The Week of Firsts

It is the *first* of June, and there are many *firsts* on my mind. *First* of all, this has been one of the most unusual weeks of my life.

The *first* traffic accident of my life occurred when I got to Saigon. There was my *first* admission to a hospital as an adult and especially without any serious physical complications. The *first* visit to a nonhostile foreign country. The *first* time to visit an island named Penang. The *first* time to check into a hotel without my parents or anyone else I know. The *first* time to feel so dirty in a clean tourist-focused environment. The *first* time to take a shower then a bath—then a shower then a bath— then a shower (that must have been the *first* time it took a full two plus hours to feel sanitized enough to be in public surroundings).

This week was the *first* time to leave a hotel room and go to a hotel bar and then order for the *first* time peppermint schnapps. It was certainly the *first* time ever to be approached by a good-looking female and be asked by her, "What are you doing for the next few days?" She told me it was her *first* time to take a week off from her normal activities and associations with R&R military personnel.

It was an enjoyable *first* time to eat lobster, and the lobster was so big that the tail must have measured around 12 inches. Also, it was the *first* time to be measured for a custom-made suit to be sent home. It was also the *first* time an R&R service member went surfing at the north end of the island, and I didn't need a wetsuit. Eating, buying, and surfing measured up to a great time that suited me fine.

Upon returning to Saigon, I must have been the *first* Navy low-ranking guy to ever get a double seat by myself in an Army Jeep in an Army convoy riding in the *first* vehicle in a dust-generating entourage of Army equipment. That occurred because I was the *first* one to respond "Yes!" to "Does anyone know how to operate a 50-caliber machine gun?"

Yes, there was another *first*. But that is the *last* thing I would ever write about.

Jun 5, 1968 – It's Time to Tell

It's time to write my parents to tell them what I wrote to Jacquie, telling her what I want for our future.

05 Jun '68

Dear Folks,

I know it's been a while since I wrote, but I have my reasons. But before I tell them, I have an announcement to make. I just wrote Jacquie to tell her to tell her folks that I plan on marrying her upon my return. I've put a lot of thought and prayer into it, and I have my decision. I love her, and I know what I'm doing.

My reasons for not writing. Well, I just got back from R&R. I left on the 24th of May from the boats and proceeded to Saigon. On the 25th, I left the country and headed for six days and five nights in Penang. What a place! Had a wonderful time. I bought a tailor-made suit and vest with extra contrasting pants and vest, all for $75. I mailed them 4th class, so it will be a while before you receive them. When you do, would you put them away and in October have them cleaned and pressed? That reminds me. You can expect me home in November, near the middle.

While trying to get back to where I'm stationed, I had to ride a few Army convoys. I was shotgun for one, but nothing happened. It surprised a lot of the Army guys to see a Navy man as gunner on a Jeep.

I didn't know I was going on R&R until the 23rd of May. It was a rush-rush thing. Well, it's time to run. I've got some errands to do, so bye for now.

Love,
Tom

The letter to my parents will make much more sense if I include this entry about what I wrote Jacquie:

My Dearest Jacquie,

I guess you can see that I have addressed this letter a little bit differently than the previous letters. First, I want to thank you for allowing me to write you and for writing me back. When I volunteered for Vietnam, I never expected to return home, but now things and especially my feelings have changed. You are on my mind constantly, and I am overwhelmed by the desire to be with you. I don't know whether I will survive this year, and if I do, I don't know whether I will come home a complete man. I do know I want to spend my life with you. At this point, I certainly want to live.

Even though we both have had a few rough times, I truly believe we were meant for each other. With those thoughts in my heart, I hope and pray that you will be waiting for me when I return, and I hope and pray that you will be my wife.

I do love you!

Love,
Tom

PS: I hope you will share this with your parents.

Jun 10, 1968 – Difficult Times

Getting a break from combat does not make combat any easier. I can't help but think about King David, King Saul, and Saul's son, Jonathan. They had an intertwining difficult relationship. Combat and battles played a significant role in their relationship triad. We just had a visitation by a high-ranking admiral whose father was a pioneer of aircraft carrier operations. He has been deemed the new commander of the Pacific forces (CINCPAC). He entered the United States Naval Academy at age 16 and spent much of his four years in contention with authority and working off massive doses of extra duty. He graduated in 1931, finishing 423rd out of 441 in class rank. While stationed in Long Beach, California, he met a gal, and they eloped to Tijuana, Mexico, to get married (against her parents' wishes). He was suspended five days for leaving his ship without permission. Today, he is giving awards to some brave sailors for combat valor. At the same time, his son is a prisoner of war, if he is still alive. His son was shot down a few months ago on a mission over North Vietnam. I don't understand how such a leader can smile while contemplating the future and the condition of his son. I hope he, his son, and the rest of us can get through these very difficult times. I think the Admiral's last name is Cain or something like that.

Jun 16, 1968 – The Two Questions

My brother has written a letter describing the social and political unrest that is occurring in Riverside and throughout the nation. He is well-read, extremely intelligent, and very thoughtful about the complexities of life. He has analytical capabilities of gathering information from a multitude of sources and is adept at reading between the lines and making good summations about what he investigates. Because he works for the US Navy, he knows a lot about the Mobile Riverine Force and its functions and operations but does not share all the information with our parents. He has asked me two very penetrating questions that I have been thinking about during the past few days.

Question number one: "Are you still feeling 'okay' about your decision to go to Vietnam in a combat role?" My original decision to come to Vietnam and be involved in combat had to do with not wanting to live, but John and my parents do not know that. A portion of my thoughts about not living originated from my admiration of my brother's goals, plans, and intellectual capabilities. I could not see myself being able to reach his potential achievements. My reason for being here has changed from "not wanting to live" to wanting to "live for the future." I am hoping that I can do my part for the future of the citizens of Vietnam, so I am okay with coming here.

Question number two: "Do you think the US involvement in Vietnam is worthwhile?" I don't know anything about politics and international relations. I do know that America has wonderful freedoms that others should be able to experience. Is it worthwhile for some to die so others can be free? It must be, or else there would be no United States.

Since we are on a long cruise of approximately 18 hours, I think I will write a letter home and answer my brother's questions.

Jun 16, 1968 – A Letter to Home

Dear Folks,

Sorry for delays in my letter writing, but life has been busy here. Ever since returning from R&R, we've had a full load of work. I've never worked so hard in all my life, but things are getting back to normal now.

It's funny that you didn't get a letter before you got the package I mailed. I mailed them both on the same day, and there shouldn't have been any duty on it.

Well, John, it's hard for me to comprehend that you have graduated from UCR. It doesn't seem like you've been in college that long. But I must say I'm pretty proud of you. If you can remember the two questions in the letter you wrote me, the answers are "yes."

Well, it's time for me to close. The boat is in transit, and it's my turn to drive, so bye for now.

Love,
Tom

Jun 30, 1968 – Who? Read That Letter

Well, well, well. Life has some strange curveballs.

My Dearest Tom,

I really like the way you started such a special letter. It stirred up a lot of memories of our past. Just like you said, there have been some rough spots, but I want to focus on some of the great times we have cherished. I remember the song titled "Cherish" that The Association sang at the grad night party that I went to but didn't stay with Roy and chose to be with you. I guess that did upset him a little, and then the next night, we went to Ramona's all-nighter, and the next night we went to the church's all-nighter in Chinatown, and then we went on that date and fell asleep. Our parents sure got upset about us not getting home till 3 in the morning, and I know your parents accused you of what we did not do.

I didn't like the idea of you joining the Navy, but I think that was a good choice since I was leaving for college here in Conway. I must admit I was a little upset but proud of you when I took my spring break and came back from Arkansas and spent some time with you at that apartment in San Diego.

When I was getting ready to go to class yesterday, the guy I met here and who has asked me to marry him brought your letter to me. Since I was brushing my hair, I asked him to read your letter. I had no idea what it was about.

When he finished, my fiancé asked me what I planned to do. I had to tell him the truth, so I told him I'm going home to California and will be there when you return. I love you,

Tom, and I do want to spend the rest of our lives together. I will be waiting for your return whether it's all of you or not.

My deepest love!
Jacquie

Who am I to disagree?

Jul 4, 1968 – "Defence of Fort M'Henry" by F. S. Key

I witnessed several fireworks shows as a youth. It is interesting to note that my family spent many a July 4th in Arkansas where Independence Day wasn't really celebrated because of residual feelings from the intrusion by the North, but lots of fireworks were expended "just because." I have also witnessed numerous nighttime firefights when rockets have been fired and the air has streaks of red, green, and white from tracer rounds fired by all participants. I have even seen the sky light up when an ammo supply dump was ignited by a VC mortar round. But nothing compares to what has occurred this evening, except possibly what Francis Scott Key saw on the evening of September 12, 1814. All of humanity and every nation have a July 4th on the world's standard calendar, but only America celebrates it as Independence Day by lighting up the sky with anything they can. The American troops here in Vietnam have lit up our earthly cosmos with anything and everything available. I would venture to guess that I have witnessed a million-dollar explosive sight. Key's words make perfect sense to those who know.

> *O! say can you see, by the dawn's early light,*
> *What so proudly we hail'd at the twilight's last gleaming,*
> *Whose broad stripes and bright stars through the perilous fight,*
> *O'er the ramparts we watch'd, were so gallantly streaming?*
> *And the rockets' red glare, the bombs bursting in air,*
> *Gave proof through the night that our flag was still there—*
> *O! say, does that star-spangled banner yet wave*
> *O'er the land of the free, and the home of the brave?*

The answer to his last question in that verse of his poem is a resounding, colorful, sparkling, and dynamic "yes!"

Jul 9, 1968 – Thumpity Thump Thump Thump

Thumpity, thump, thump—thump! Thumpity, thump, thump—thump! It was the sound of something hitting the bottom of the boat. It plays over and over and over again—in my head. I am now the official cox'n of the boat. Robert, our previous cox'n, is now a boat captain of RivDiv 91's medical evacuation boat. He is the boatswain's mate. I am just a radioman. He knows how to tie nautical knots, establish a bosin's chair for ship-to-ship transfer, set a rigging, and all those other things a real sailor knows how to do. I just talk on a radio and share information (and a few other things). Now, I have the task of maintaining the appropriate distance between Tango 91-4 and the boat in front of us. That is not always easy, especially at nighttime.

In the cox'n flat, you face forward while standing behind the helm (steering wheel). There is a pedestal that holds the wooden steering device, engine gauges, and engine control levers. The cubicle is surrounded by armor plating. The upper front and sides have plating on hinges so they can be folded down or up. The steel plates measure 1" x 2' x 3'. The metal slats have a total of four cutouts measuring approximately 1" x 1', evenly distributed (2 by 2—across, up and down) near the center. The slabs of armor and their thin viewing slots are approximately 2 feet away from the cox'n's head. About 30 feet away, at the front of the boat, is the ramp with metal rails for traversing in and out of the well deck when the ramp is lowered. When driving, you have to look through them. At nighttime, lights of any kind are a no-no. "Can someone tell me where the boat in front is?" Bump! "Oops! Sorry 'bout that." Talk about bumps in the road, tons of tonnage hitting tons of tonnage can rattle anyone to the bones.

During the day, it is fairly easy to see the boat in front and see the view to the sides of the boat. During combat convoys, we are not allowed to vary our speed and must maintain the distance between boats no matter what. *No matter what!* What about? Just what about that little sampan that isn't supposed to go between two boats? What about the little family in it?

Thumpity, thump, thump—thump! Thumpity, thump, thump—thump! The sight of the sampan disappearing from my frontal view and the sound of something hitting the bottom of the boat will never be forgotten. It plays over and over and over again in my head. Thank you, Lord, for your grace of *forgiveness*.

Jul 12, 1968 – Where Do You Go?

I have made a commitment to go home and get married. I have also made a commitment to go home and pick up my new super-duper Datsun 240Z. Earlier, I had a chance to put some money down on the "Z car" at the Dong Tam Exchange. I guess I need to go to the Exchange and cancel my car purchase and instead go and purchase a diamond ring. It's time to go and do the right thing.

When my brother wrote and told me about the discord of opinions and actions about Vietnam, he mentioned that many guys were going out and burning their draft cards and draft notices. After they did their burning, they chose to go to Canada to avoid any and all commitment about going into the US Armed Forces. When I turned 18, I was supposed to sign up at the draft board, but I didn't go. I didn't go because I had already committed by joining the Navy.

A little while ago, we were told to have someone go to mail call and retrieve what was available for any of the boat crew members. When Gomer returned with our envelopes and packages, he said I would need to go and create a creative answer to one of my letters. The local draft board thought it was time for me to go into the Army and had sent me a notice to go and report as instructed. Now, I have to think where I should go. Should I go home and answer their call, or should I go to Canada and ignore it all? It's time to go and do the right thing. I have made a commitment. Go get a match and burn my draft notice. Let's see how far that goes!

Jul 14, 1968 – Leonardo da Vinci

Dear Folks,

Once again I am long overdue for writing you a letter. I am doing fine and dandy, couldn't be better. I'm excited about coming home in five months or so. It does make me feel good to know that y'all have given Jacquie and me your blessings. I can't wait to take her as my wife. Although it's going to be hard to set up a wedding because of my being so far away and not knowing exactly when I'll be home, I'm sure everything will turn out all right.

I should probably account for my not writing due to being busy. Let me paint you a picture. Typically in a month's time, we spend about 300 hours underway either on patrol or operations. In the last four weeks, we have clocked about 450 hours on patrol and painted our boat (top to bottom, front to back, left to right, in and out, and up and down). It took 13 gallons of flat green, one gallon of a special green, 3 gallons of nonskid, one gallon of varnish, 5 gallons of grey, 5 gallons of red lead (used to prevent rust), 2 gallons of red, 2 gallons of white, and a little bit of blue and yellow for our boat name sign. We have covered more ground (water) in the last month than we did during the first six months of being in the country.

I have got to get back to painting, so goodbye for now.

Love,
Tom

Jul 21, 1968 – Satisfaction

What is life when there is no satisfaction from it? I know of three entities that have approached such a complicated situation. The three have such diversity. What do King Solomon, Porter Wagoner, and the Rolling Stones have in common? On the surface, not much, but an in-depth survey reveals they proclaim the key to life is finding *satisfaction*. Fighting for your life, fighting for the lives of others, and finding a commonality between you and others give meaning to life that cannot be defined by simple words or concepts. I have lost friends and don't even know who they were. I have gained friends and don't know who they are. To live in a place of death is very unsatisfying. But to live is satisfying, and I choose to be satisfied.

Jul 27, 1968 – Ooh! Rats!

I have heard that the noise level in prison is very loud. Could that noise level be louder than living on these boats? As I previously wrote, the engines are always running, and many people are always awake and shouting back and forth plus playing any kind of music as loud as possible. The ships also generate numerous types of sounds and audible disruptions. There is the whoop-whoop-whoop of helicopters, frequent cannon gunfire and firefights in the surrounding vicinity, the obnoxious snoring of someone sleeping, and of course, the "Sound of Silence." The words from the 1966 release by Simon and Garfunkel loudly whisper in the echoes of my mind and create my own thoughts.

Singing about darkness being a friend
softly creeping visions while sleeping
and about a vision remaining planted in my brain,
all occurring during the sound of silence.

The last time I was sleeping, I was dreaming about getting a pedicure. I have never had a pedicure. I have no memory or recollection or information about what a pedicure would be like. This pedicure dream woke me from my sleep because my right big toe was being chewed on by a critter. This critter was about the size of a cat or opossum. Critters are known for swimming from the shore to the boats and ships and trying to create an environment where they can live. We do have a solution to help reduce the critter infiltration.

Parts of the boat's armament are the shotguns. Most of the shotguns are short barreled so they can be used in self-defense against human intruders. If you take a shotgun's round shell apart, you can remove the pellets inside. Once the pellets are gone, it can only shoot out the wadding that has been left. A shotgun round with just the wad is reasonably harmless to the surrounding area and human users. However, the round is still very deadly to invading critters when shot at a point-blank range. Our 25 boats can kill a hundred critters in a night.

I don't think this activity of killing critters is the meaning for "a shot in the dark," but I do know it's another noise in the night—the reason many call us "The River Rats."

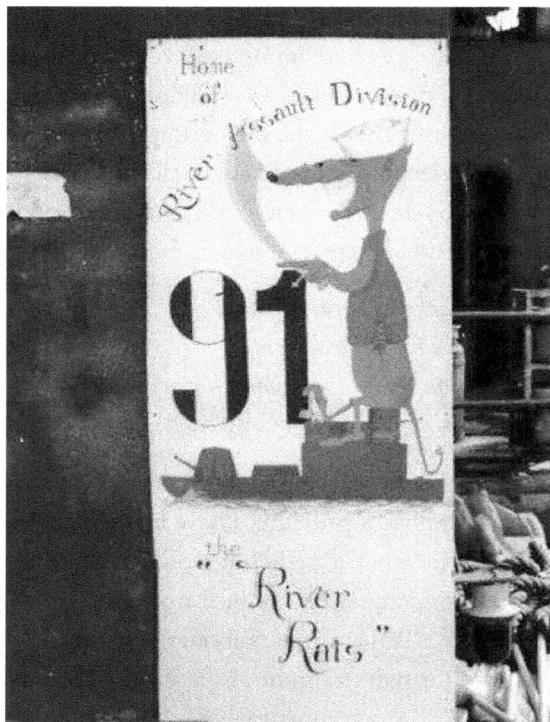

River Rats poster

Aug 2, 1968 – The Gift

Yesterday we started a long transit to an area where the US military has not been. While in route, a boat behind us lost use of a rudder and could not maneuver correctly in the canal we were using for our excursion. A tow line was hooked up from Tango 4, and we towed it.

We were informed on the monitor in front of us that a *National Geographic* magazine photographer was traveling with our combat force. He was there to take pictures for a magazine article about the Mekong Delta scheduled for the December 1968 issue. During the all-night drive (relieve yourself while staying in place), I had trouble maintaining a correct directional position and assumed it was because of the boat that was being towed. Shortly after sunrise, the Viet Cong decided to give us a welcoming surprise. We returned their surprise when we opened up with everything we had. They did manage to inflict significant damage to several boats, including Tango 4. The explosion from one of the rocket rounds the VC shot managed to give my legs a few gifts of metal souvenirs (shrapnel). Once their surprise party was over and we found a safe location to survey all damage to boats, it was discovered that one of my rudders was also broken. I bet this 20th birthday will not be forgotten.

Aug 2, 1968 – Part 2

Dear Tommy,

There are times when one turns back the time and relives some of the fond memories gone by, and that's what I'm doing. Twenty years ago, I was waiting expectantly for you to arrive. I was hoping for a boy, but Daddy wanted a girl (he changed his mind when you got here, though – he had bought you a baby doll). Then it was time for your arrival.

When you and I went home from the hospital, Daddy had a rocking chair waiting for us. You were such a good baby and didn't need rocking, but you and I spent a lot of time rocking because we both enjoyed it.

Many nights I would wake you up just to hold, rock, or play with you. You were a joy and comfort to me when Daddy was working and John was sound asleep.

As the years began to go by, you didn't change but remained a special boy in my life and many others, too. You seem to have a personality that is a real fine gift, that of being able to enjoy people of all ages. I have never heard you criticize or gripe about people.

I found it hard when you grew up and knew that you would soon no longer be my little boy. I wasn't always the mother you deserved, but being a parent isn't easy, and perhaps my mistakes will help you do a better job than I did.

Now you are twenty, having experienced many things, and it's my prayer that the years ahead will be happy ones, and my heart holds so much love for you.

Happy Birthday,
Your Mom

Aug 9, 1968 - Collateral Damage

The Mekong Delta has numerous subordinate rivers, tributaries, and canals. Regrettably, the Delta area has many characteristics similar to a septic system. A septic system has laterals. The word *lateral* comes from Latin *lateralis*, which means "belonging to the side." They disperse human waste outward. Here, the laterals also collect human waste. If I borrow money and have something to offer as collateral, it means the other entity may not lose anything because we each have side-by-side vested interest in the exchange.

Yesterday, August the 8th, we finally finished a long and extensive operation south of the city of Can Tho. Most units had experienced an exchange of fire as we traversed through a particular area when the operation began. When we approached the exit from the operation area, the exchange occurred again. River Division 92 was in a firefight that left 29 citizens killed and 27 wounded. Two hours later, River Division 91 was in an ambush at the same location, and an ATC was beached to keep it from sinking. One hour later, the artillery barges, with Riverine boat escorts, arrived in our exchange (firefight) location and came under attack also. They had—and fired—1,000 rounds of 105 Howitzer "beehive" ammunition. (A beehive Howitzer round is like a 5" shotgun round full of darts, and it will pin people against a wall or a tree.) So all the river boats opened, and the net results were 42 civilians killed, one ARVN killed, and 177 wounded with 15 being ARVN soldiers.

Now, I know the meaning of collateral damage.

Aug 12, 1968 – Sous-Chefs

We Riverine sailors are not just pawns or peons; we are a very unique class of sous-chefs. Sous-chefs are in charge of making sure cooking equipment is in working order. We must be certain that the cardboard boxes that contain C-rats (combat rations) are available for open-fire cooking and that mini-toilet paper rolls are handy as extra fuel.

There must be plenty of C-4 (formable explosive plastic) available to make large marble-sized balls for speed cooking. We have to be sure the engines are running so some items can cook slowly or always be ready for a hasty meal. We must thoroughly understand how to use and troubleshoot all cooking instruments in the event of a malfunctioning cooking device.

Sous-chefs need to be responsive and have the ability to improvise when a problem arises, and we must also ensure safety precautions and sanitary provisions are taken to ensure a safe and clean working environment. We regularly wash the boat with the Mekong River water. High-end chefs are responsible for inventory, product and supply rotation, and menu tasting. Thankfully, the Tabasco Company published the *Charlie Ration Cookbook* with tasty ideas about how to adapt C-rats into gourmet meals. We even know how to make a chocolate birthday cake from contents of the C-rats packages. For the sake of flavor, we put Tabasco sauce on everything.

Aug 15, 1968 – Green and Brown

It's all green and brown—brown water, brown food, brown dead bodies, brown bathwater, brown vest, brown skin—theirs and ours—green paint, green clothes, green surroundings except for the brown, green clothes not regulation (green Levi's cut off). Ham and eggs are green, too—puke green—green replacements (don't know who they are or how long they have been with us on the boat and don't care). We are a five-man team (but Robert is the captain of the medical boat), should be seven, down two, really three, we are six (who were the fifth and sixth men? One must have been the current boat captain).

We are turning left at the Crossroads. Usually we go right, and we have been to this area before. We got our tail shot off last April. If it wasn't for this war, this would be a beautiful sight. Ignore the smells of body odor, diesel fuel, the typical aromas of the streams and side villages, defecation, rotting stuff, cooking things that are different. The brown water has fishnets strung across the stream (or canal, don't know the difference right now). I know those nets are and will be a problem. Zigzag, we are past them. The shooting starts, it must be late afternoon, we push to the landing sites—ambush slows us down, some boats are taking serious hits, tide goes out.

The brown mud of the banks is growing higher. We bank as the sun goes down. Troops are unloaded. They plant a perimeter in front of us. All boats remain on one side of the stream, Army in front, Navy guns pointed to the rear. The smell of diesel and sulfur is heavy in the air. We get word we're spending the night in this place. That's scary. Army is just beyond the lowered ramps—they need grenades, pass cases to them, throw and explode, throw and explode. The noise is loud, not as loud as the gun battle to get here. There's a place in the back of the boat to take a nap (where Gomer likes to hide). It's been hours of gun ordinance exchange; maybe one or two hours of rest will help. I smell stink—body odor, my vest, lousy food, thick vegetation.

Aug 16, 1968 – Cursing God

The sun comes up. It is not brown or green but a very beautiful rainbow hue of mist. The tide is coming in—promises of getting out of here. We are heading back to the Crossroads. I see them again, the nets.

We have been under fire for a long, long time. More and more boats are taking serious hits. The Huey gunships and the bombers have joined the escapade. How can we be this close to bombs and rockets going off and still be under enemy fire? Got to go left, swing pass the net, swing right, head for the bank so I can turn left. That second boat ahead of us is making its turn to the left to make its course toward the Crossroads intersection. That VC is standing up and firing a round (RPG type). It landed in the water but amidships. How did he do that with boat gunfire, gunships shooting, and those bombers? This is scary. This is desperate! "Guys, shoot toward the starboard bank!" The boat in front has just turned left; she is in front of the rocketeer. He stands, he shoots, the rocket hits amidships at the waterline. Damn! Damn! Damn! He should be dead. Didn't that last bomb just land on top of him? How did he do that? "Shoot to the starboard!"—say it many times. When I swing to the left, I'll be in his sights *This is what you came here for.* You know Charlie shoots for the cox'n flat. You're the cox'n, hear the gunfire, the bombs, the shouting from radios with people screaming.

Make the turn. "Shoot to the starboard!" What a noise! Instantly black—everything—sound, light, being. Am I okay? Am I alive? I know I have feet. I have hands. I have a steering wheel to operate. What happened? He got us! But not me. Crap! Turn my head. I have never seen three men tied in a human granny knot. "Gomer, get up here!" They're mangled. Frank, you look like you're dead.

I yell on the radio "We've been hit!" Another bomb is exploding on top of his position. "How many are wounded?" squawks the radio. "I think all of us." I know I am—arm and leg hits, Gomer's bleeding,

Frank and the other two gunners, and the boat captain, well—"I need a medevac." The smell of blood is overwhelming. Drive, drive, drive!! It's scary. The tango landing top is dropping back, coming alongside. Charlie's still shooting. A chopper is landing on the tango flattop. People (Army and Navy) are tying us up, Frank is being passed over to the flat top, bombs are going off, we are all still shooting. Well, not Tango 4.

The gauntlet is run. I hear on the radio the word is being passed to all the boats in the Delta vicinity to idle as they near our convoy. We are sinking, nine out of 16 boats. There's the Crossroads. Beach the boat, climb out of the cox'n flat, stand on the side of it, point my finger toward heaven, and scream, "Damn You, God!"

I know my Lord can and will forgive me. But for now, I will live a life in stupid rebellion.

Aug 17, 1968 – Letter from John

Dear Tom,

I just wanted to let you know about yesterday. I woke up and began to get ready to go to work. On coming out of my room, I was surprised to discover that Mom was already up. She and Dad usually got up just before I left for work. She was sitting at the dining shelf in the kitchen drinking a cup of coffee. I spoke to her a couple of times before she realized I was there. She was then startled to see me. She was obviously spooked out. I asked her about it.

She took a few moments to begin. She had been up for a few hours. In the middle of the night, about 2:00 or 3:00 a.m., she was awakened by a dream, a vivid dream. It was sort of like a nightmare but not. She was in a space full of noise, sounds, colors, smells. There was a cloudy fog, but it was not fog. It was gray, spots of greenish, spots of brownish, short flickers of red, and short flashes of bright light. The noise was overwhelming with growls, short staccato, and then some big loud booming sounds.

This was all very overwhelming for her. I noticed that as she lifted her cup to sip, she reached around with her other hand to rub the back upper part of her arm above her elbow. She did this another time, and I asked her about it. She commented that she must have banged or scraped her arm before she woke up fully.

I waited for a while and left for work a little late. Mom seemed to be calm when I left, but she still seemed distant. I called her during the day to see how she was doing. She said she was okay. When I got home, she still seemed overwhelmed but doing fine more or less.

I hope everything is okay.

Love.

John

Aug 18, 1968 – Diamond in the Rough

I have to admit the last few days have been rather ragged and rough. Frank is going to live, but apparently, he will have a few parts possibly missing and some other related damage. In the last four days, there have been at least five firefights involving River Division 91 and River Division 112. Three sailors have been killed, 55 have been wounded, and one is missing in action. The Army has also suffered some significant losses.

> *The Crossroads booth has a charge of toll,*
> *It doesn't matter which way you go,*
> *You choose to go left, right, ahead, or turn back,*
> *Just try your best to choose the right track.*

I have a strong need to write home and let them know a little about what is going on in my world.

18 Aug '68

Dear Folks,

Well, I have some important news to tell you, but I don't want you to worry because nothing is really wrong. I got slightly wounded two days ago, but it's only a little scratch on my arm. It will heal in a couple of days. Also, I am a little sick, mostly tired, so I'm on bed rest for a couple of days.

Time is getting short. Less than four months to go. I'm sorry about not writing as often as I used to, but life is changing. It's getting busier all the time. But time goes faster.

You won't be receiving any money this month for the savings account. I'm afraid I bought something for Jacquie. But it will be a while before I receive it, so she won't be able to get it until I'm home.

Well, there's not much more to write about, so I'll close for now.

Until later.

Love,
Tom

I wonder why I didn't tell them more about the engagement ring.

Sep 1, 1968 – Oliver Twist

When I hear the phrase "what the dickens," it is natural to assume that it might be related to Charles Dickens. But it is not. It is related to Shakespearean writings and is another way of saying "what the f. . ." Charles Dickens and either phrase bring to mind my friend Ollie. He is the 20 mm cannon gunner on Tango 91-3. I have previously mentioned that Ollie is short for Oliver Twist, which is our version of the gunner's real name, Andy Twist. Ollie is a true hero. He does like to use "what the f . . . " phrase a lot.

Many of us have obtained the new little electronic device that uses 3-inch reel-to-reel tapes for recordings. Ollie decided to record a firefight that we had a few days ago. In the recording, you can hear his weapon firing and then stop, and Ollie starts using his favorite phrase. Minutes later, his weapon again starts firing. Not only does it fire but he manages to shoot a stream of maybe 100+ rounds. In reality, the weapon should be fired only two to five rounds (ideally three) at a time, pause, then let it cool down a little bit. That's not Ollie's style. When he does something, he does it all the way with everything he has. During the firefight, I saw his barrel turn white-hot. As he moved his gun mount while shooting, it took a moment for the barrel to follow the movement. The barrel was bending as he shot. When the firefight was over, it was nothing for him to disassemble the barrel, throw it into the river, and replace it with a new one. I know the barrels cost several thousand dollars each.

Ollie is not twisted. He is a straight shooter whom I admire, and yesterday, he was given a silver star for his brave actions on April 4th when he pulled so many soldiers from the river—*in the middle of a firefight.*

Sep 5, 1968 – Up Yours, Snoopy!

I think just about everyone loves the Peanuts character known as Snoopy. All of us here do. He has an enemy known as the flying Red Baron. We have an enemy that is known for flyin' a flag bearin' red on it, and they can always be found at a particular place. Many firefights have occurred in the area known as the Crossroads, but just as deadly is a place known as Snoopy's Nose. Back in January when the Tet Offensive started, we were keeping the peace up that nose. In September 1967, a little before I arrived, there was a major battle at the location. During 0730–1600 hours on 15 September, the boats used 10,273 rounds of 40 mm cannon ammunition, 16 rounds of 81 mm mortars, 7,445 rounds of 20 mm cannon (machine gun), 20,934 rounds of .50-caliber, and 40,216 rounds of .30-caliber. Who knows how many M-16 and M-60 rounds were shot. The battle began when Tango 91-4 was damaged by a mine. When the operation ended, the Mobile Riverine Force had suffered 16 killed and 146 wounded, and the Viet Cong had suffered 213 dead.

This afternoon, we were up Snoopy's Nose retrieving some Army soldiers and taking them back to the Riverine base. We got into a little skirmish with our Red enemy. Six sailors were wounded.

I have several weapons in the cox'n flat. When I saw a Viet Cong pop his head up, like the one that did it on the 16th of August, I didn't wait for our gunners to shoot at him. I decided I would. I grabbed an M-16, raised it up to the top of the armor plating, and fired a few rounds. Based on what I saw, even if it wasn't my rounds that hit him, he was definitely hit. That flying red splatter mist is unmistakable, so . . . "up yours!"

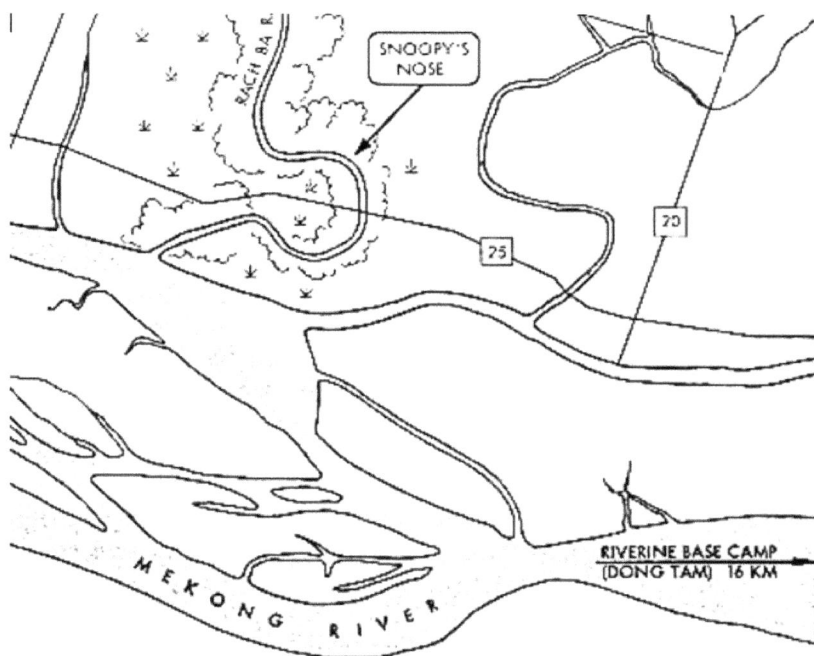

From John A. Cash, John Albright, and Allan W. Sandstrum, *Seven Firefights in Vietnam.* *Courtesy Office of the Chief of Military History, United States Army, Washington, DC, 1985,* Library of Congress Catalog Card Number 71-605212.

Sep 15, 1968 – Camaraderie

It is written in 1 Corinthians 15:26, "The last enemy that shall be destroyed is death." From this Bible passage, two famous writers wrote about death. John Donne of "No Man Is an Island" wrote Devine Meditation 10, "Death Be Not Proud," and William Shakespeare wrote "Sonnet 146." The loss of a friend, companion, or associate can occur so quickly and somewhat in the simplest simplicity. Death is just one way for a loss to occur. There is a visual image that continually occurs in my mind. A few days ago, after a firefight with the enemy, we were all standing on top of our boats surveying them for any possible damage and at the same time relaxing and, in a friendly way, shouting back and forth. A friend, the 20 mm gunner on a Tango boat, rested his hand on the end of his barrel as he stood next to it. What caused that machine gun cannon to fire is unknown, but what that machine gun cannon fire caused is known. It caused a loss—a loss of a hand, a loss of a comrade, a loss of peacefulness in a violent environment.

After I lost the camaraderie of my friend Frank, he was replaced by a fellow named Sammy. Sammy is easy to be around and has a smile that just melts your heart. Currently, I don't even know my boat captain, nor do I know the other 50-caliber machine gun gunner. Frank was able to talk me into smoking a little marijuana because he thought I was fighting depression. He may have been right, but all I know is that when I woke up the next morning, nothing had changed. If Sammy wanted me to join him in partaking, I would probably do so—just because.

Being comrades facing death together creates a bond that goes beyond death. Death, where is thy victory?

Sep 18, 1968 – A Song from Solomon

Because of my dad's musical talents with his Martin guitar and my mom's enjoyment of music, I have had a special relationship with music. As I sit here in combat conditions in the middle of the night, the music flows through my thoughts and creates the emotions and feelings that stir my hand to write. Solomon wrote Ecclesiastes 3, and I know he wrote it just for me. I know I must live for today because the future will certainly be an eve of destruction.

My admiration for Barry McGuire of the New Christy Minstrels has been replaced by his replacement, a fellow named Kenny Rogers. I hope he does well. A year ago or so, The Association came out with a new song that was unlike the previous ones. It struck a chord that cannot be described. "Requiem for the Masses" seemed to hold a premonition for my future. There is a hope and a dream that it is not—that has been a major change from why I wanted to serve in this environment. Now I hope we can do something good for this country and that it won't turn out like so many back home are proclaiming that it will. Pete Seeger has written it best, using Solomon's words and The Byrds' vocals. I just hope things "Turn! Turn! Turn!"

Sep 20-ish, 1968 – Military Artillery Facilitatory Allegory

I am not sure when this happened, I just know that it did.
The enemy was shooting all around us, and there was not a place where our boat could be hid.
The commanding colonel was directing arty fire from a helicopter up above.
Flying around, darting here and there, getting a bird's eye view just like a dove.
He called for a salvo of rounds to hit the enemy where they traverse,
Never realizing what he had done could not have been worse.
One round flew toward us, hitting our boat's light mast,
Causing me to yell out a curse—"You're hitting us but not the enemy you plan."
"I don't like what you're doing, I don't give a damn."
He told me I was wrong, but I knew I had more insight,
So I told him where to go so he could see we were in his arty sight.
The arty rounds stopped when I heard his helicopter flight,
It was at the same time he realized I was right.
Sailor to colonel protocol went out the window
The day arty rounds came in way too low.

Sep 22, 1968 – Times Are Changin'

Where did the good old times go?
Can anybody really know?
We run around and go around
Hoping that the old can be found.
Have to find a way to look to the future
And bind the old wounds with a suture.

In three months, December 22, I will be married. Nine months ago, I was headed out to an operation for the Christmas Peacekeeping Truce to die in a blaze of glory. I guess, as Bob Dylan says, "The times they are a-changin." Makes me think about my friends, the twins, Paul and Steve, and how they loved Dylan's songs, especially "Rainy Day Women."

Bobby Kennedy and Martin Luther King, Jr. have lost their lives. The new home run slugger, rookie Bobby Bonds, a PE locker neighbor from my seventh grade, is the new grand slam hero. On the boat, only three original crew members remain, and Sammy, Frank's replacement, has been sent to be the gunner of the 40 mm cannon of a monitor. Some of our field food is being replaced by something new, and regularity (bowel-type) is gone. (Someone might be conducting an experiment with us because they think we are rats—river-type.) The new Monitor boats have 105 mm Howitzers, sawed-off short barrels on them, and all the new Tangos have flat tops for helicopters. And the new music—seems more angry.

Oct 3, 1968 – Uncivil War

It is becoming harder and harder to write home, partly because I'm trying to use a little new electronic device that records my voice on a 3" reel that I can send home and receive spoken "letters" back. But another reason is because the only topic to write about is the war experience that is occurring all around. Thanks to my dad, I at least know that what I am experiencing is not that unusual. He was going through his deceased dad's stuff and found a copy of a letter, which he mailed to me. It reads:

Camp near Richmond (Virginia)
June the 1st, 1862

Dear Mary:

Your letter of the 23rd was received, and it afforded me a great deal of pleasure to hear from you and hear that you and Tomey and Eddy was well, and the rest of the family and kindred. I am well and as hearty as a hog. I have nothing to write, only about the war.

There was a battle commenced yesterday morning about 7 miles below where we are, and they fought all day and all night and are still fighting yet. We have heavy losses—two or three killed—General Johnson severely wounded. General McGruder wounded. General Tatnell and General Petigrew killed. No further particulars of the battle, but it will be ended today.

There was a large body of the Yankees crossed Chickominy River, and the bridge washed away and they could not get back, and our men attacked them. Our loss is some 3 or 4 thousand—the Yankees loss is not known. We took about 25,000 prisoners and 11 batteries and some small arms.

We are now in the edge of the battlefield and expecting a fight every day. The battle was fought 5 miles from Richmond. Since I started this letter, we had to move, and Johnson is not only slightly wounded, so I must close for want of time.

Mary, I would more than be glad to get to come home and see you all, but I can't get out of camp at all. But I think that the war will soon close, if I should live to see it, and I hope I shall. Give my love and respects to all our kindred and inquiring friends, and receive yourself my most true and affectionate love from your obedient husband.

James W. Center

My brother has previously told me about our multi-great grandpa and how he was a sharpshooter (sniper) but died at Gettysburg. I have to wonder whether he was one of the fellows who fought against my all-time hero, Joshua Lawrence Chamberlain, known as a Hero of Gettysburg who held Little Round Top at all hazards.

Oct 14, 1968 – Tammy

I will be home in less than two months. It's October 14th, and we are going back "on line." Therefore, there will be more chances to not go home in one piece. But I think what really is going to kill me is my good friend Gomer. Like Debbie Reynolds in the movie *Tammy* who sings about being in love with someone who doesn't even seem to realize she exists, Gomer seems to have the same problem. He loves country music and has a major idol crush on a young female singer named Tammy.

Someone lovingly and foolishly sent him her new release. He found a little battery-operated record player, and now he plays the song over and over and over again. When we arrived here, Gomer was the last person in the world I would choose to be around, but now life in combat and horrendous experiences have changed my feelings. I am certain that song will play forever in my head. These words of mine are similar and ring true about Gomer:

> *Words about bad times, words about good times,*
> *Him doing things that are hard to understand,*
> *And knowing him and living with him*
> *You end up forgiving him.*
> *He's very hard to understand.*
> *But when you love him, you will be proud of him*
> *Because like me, he is just a man.*
> *So the title of her song rings true,*
> *"Stand by Your Man."*

Oct 19, 1968 – Johnny Sings

While in my journal I have been writing
And in the background the radio's playing,
Different words come to my mind
Still relating to "Walking the Line."
Johnny sings about keeping a close watch on his heart all the time.
I say, "I think you've been reading my mind."
Johnny sings about keeping his eyes wide open all the time.
I say, "That's something to do when back on line."
Johnny sings about keeping the tie that binds.
I say, "I will love you till the end of time."
Johnny sings about it being very easy to be true.
I say, "I really can't find a way to disagree with you."
Johnny sings about being alone when each day's through.
I say, "I feel so alone and feel kind of blue."
Johnny sings about admitting he's a fool for you.
I say, "I am thinking I feel that way, too."
Johnny sings about night is dark and day is light.
I say, "What seems loose is sometimes chokingly tight."
Johnny sings about keeping you on his mind both day and night.
I say, "I never want you out of my sight."
Johnny sings about the happiness he's known proves it's right.
I say, "I'll work to get to you with all my might."
Johnny sings about she has a way to keep him on her side.
I say, "I'll keep going, just for the ride."
Johnny sings about a cause for love that he can't hide.
I say, "I just want to be by your side."
Johnny sings about trying to turn the tide.
I say, "No one will claim I never tried."
Johnny claims, "Because you're mine, I walk the line."
I say, "To be with you is forever fine."
And we both just walk the line.
And we both just walk the line.

Oct 27, 1968 – Apologies to Bobby Darin

We have been out on an operation for several days. A few days ago, October 24th, we had a firefight at the location where we are now. This location is currently at least fairly secure from a threat by any VC. There are ground troops all around us securing our perimeter, and we are maintaining a resupply scenario for the troops who are out and about on search and destroy operations. Sometimes, when there are firefights, combatants from either side may end up in the river because of being wounded or killed. If those bodies sink and are not immediately found, a few days later they may pop up due to gaseous decomposition.

A little while ago, I decided to take a river bath. The Mekong River delta is full of water that is used for washing away human and animal excrement from cities and villages. For instance, the bucket we have on board is our toilet and an all-purpose water tool for cleaning ourselves and the boat. You dip the bucket into the river and pour it on yourself, soap up, scrub your body, and then grab another bucket load to rinse the soap off. Well, while I was scrubbing, I decided not to rinse.

Splishin' and splashin', I was a bathin'
Long about a Sunday noon, yeah
A rub dub dub, just relaxin' with my bucket tub
Thinkin' everythin' was alright
When I saw such an ugly sight!
Well, I stepped away from my bucket tub
I put my feet on the deck
I wrapped the towel around me and
said, What the heck?
And then with a splash
I threw away my bath
Well, how was I to know
There were some dead bodies floatin' on?

Nov 11, 1968 – The Longest Day

Today is Veterans Day, and I am feeling emotionally drained and physically exhausted. We just got back from a weeklong operation called Delta Raider. We arrived in the country about 11 months ago and thought we would be rotating home by this time. "We" refers to the seven-man crew and other classmates that trained together at Mare Island. It is hard to comprehend the number of people needed to help us maintain a crew of six. Our first loss was never replaced. At last count, 23 people have been part of Tango 91-4's crew since just before Christmas. I have tried my best not to make friends for about the last six months. I especially tried to get coldhearted when my buddy Frank was shot up so bad last August, but his replacement, Sammy, had an infectious smile and an engaging personality, so we became friends.

For some reason, I have been the acting boat captain for the past few days. A boat captain sits outside the boat structure between the cox'n flat and the three gun mounts and has a fairly good view of the surrounding territory. Yesterday, that was where I was sitting when we went to the area known as the Crossroads. My friend Sammy had been transferred to Monitor 91-2. He was in charge of the 40 mm cannon on that boat. Of course, because we are at the Crossroads, we have to expect the expected, and the expected occurred—another firefight. We just had one the day before on the 9th!

The shooting started, and all hell broke loose yesterday morning. I have been in at least a hundred firefights but never have I seen one because of my usual location in the boat. Sitting in a position normally occupied by a lifer (career sailor) is totally different from just driving the boat. Bullets are whizzing, cannon rounds are exploding, and rockets are blasting their devastation. "Cease fire! Cease fire! Cease fire!" the radio proclaims. Silence that is deafening grabs the smoke-filled air that we breathe and shoves it down our throats to where our hearts are.

"Please, Mr. Custer, I don't want to go!"

"Sammy, please! Please! Get back into your gun mount. Why have you climbed out? Why are you standing there outside in plain view here at the Crossroads?" He didn't know what hit him. I do. I saw it. It is a memory I will have to live with, and I don't like it.

After the firefight and the troops landed, we started our transit to the location where they would be picked up. They would travel in a southeast direction while we traveled back west to the Crossroads, then south to another river, then east to a canal, and then north to the pickup point. Since I was an acting—and low-ranking—boat captain, a decision was made to put Tango 4 at the end of the column. The concept was quite rational because the VC loved to disable the lead boats of a convoy column, so all boats become sitting ducks ready for easy destruction. The ground troops took longer than anticipated for their travel, and our transit also took longer than originally anticipated. As we went upstream in the canal, the water level was still high, and we could look down on the banks. By the time we were able to reload the troops, ebb tide had occurred, and we were up the creek in the mud, unable to reposition the boats for the return trip out of the canal. I guess you could say I was now front and center of the convoy. Lower water heights meant you had to look up to see the top of the bank. It also meant the VC could look down to see us. In other words, they owned the high ground. No one wants their enemy to have control of the high ground.

Charlie decided to take advantage of his relative position. The firing started. Because the waterway had numerous bends and curves, it was hard to see the pathway to safety from a sitting position between the gun mounts, so the simple choice was made. I stood up. It was then easier to give directions to the cox'n. As I was yelling instructions to the boat driver, swoosh! Then a thunderous clap on the bank next to the boat occurred. A rocket exploded a few yards away and scattered debris back at the boat. A substantial amount of the debris hit my body. Within a fairly short time, the firefight gauntlet ended, and we continued our exit toward the big river.

At the larger body of water, I decided it was time to check my body for damage (it is called BDA—battle damage assessment). There was a little bit of stinging on my right arm. My biggest concern was what I had felt hit my face. I gingerly lifted my hand and fingers to my nose area to determine whether I had been seriously wounded. I felt a gooey mess where my nose should be and realized I was breathing through my mouth. I could not find my nose. By the time I did this body check, it had become dark.

Our boat dropped back to the end of the column, and I decided to go down below to have a cup of coffee and ask for a medevac. The realization of going home with significant injuries had been a possibility for 11 months. To go home disfigured in the face did not seem like a pleasant thought. Once I was down below, my fellow crewmen started laughing at me, and I angrily explained to them that they were not being very nice. Then they explained to me that I needed to get a lump of mud off my face and clean and bandage my arm.

When we got back to our Riverine base, someone turned on the radio. It was playing a new hit song, "Abraham, Martin, and John"— "but it seems the good die young." Yesterday was not June 6, 1944, but nonetheless, it was a long day—the Longest Day!

Nov 15, 1968 – First Base

I'm getting close to going home. In the game of war, life, and baseball, that is the primary objective. Get home! During this past year, my schoolmate and ballplayer Bobby Bonds did a pretty good job of getting home, especially considering he was a rookie with a grand slam home run in his first major league game. Some guys talk about getting to first base or hitting a home run when they are referring to interactions or dates with a gal. Interacting with females is a form of war. In war, you want to throw a strike at your enemy. If you strike your enemy out, they lose, and you win. Baseball is a war of two combatants—the pitcher and the batter—and it has a whole bunch of supporting roles to ensure that someone wins and someone loses.

Life is like a war. It has its winners and losers; it has its combatants—male and female—it has its objectives of getting to first base and hitting home runs. You cannot get to home if you haven't been to first base. Here at the Riverine base, the USO has hit a home run. They have sent over pitcher Pete Richert and home run hitter and first baseman Ernie Banks. Soon, I'm going home to my first base, my wife to be, Jacquie. I hope to hit a home run. But how will the game play out? Only the Great Umpire knows.

Nov 22, 1968 – Tidbits from My Last Tape Home

I want to start this tape the same way I just started one for Jacquie. Here were my first words to her: "As of 4 this morning, I finally got off the boats, and today is November 22nd, which leaves me one more month of bachelor life." I want to apologize for being so long at getting word to y'all. I made a tape for Jacquie about a week and a half to two weeks ago. I mentioned to her that I was going to make a tape for y'all. As I explained to her, things came up almost immediately, and I wasn't able to get one to y'all and haven't been able since then.

Our reliefs got in three days ago, and we've been busy breaking them in and showing them what it's like. That's why I've been unable to tell you for the last few days I was getting off.

There's an operation to the Crossroads I was supposed to have gone on with my relief, but my old boat captain put in a good word for me and said they could make it without me, so I got to stay behind. My old boat captain and cox'n is out there right now, and so is Gomer plus Roger-Dodger. Lord willing, they will be able to make it back. They won't be in for another three days.

These last three weeks have been very hectic, very busy, very hard, very tiring, very exciting, and very scary. On the last tape to Jacquie, I mentioned to her that a friend of mine, a close friend, had been killed. He was, in fact, Frank's replacement on our boat and rode with us for quite a while but then was transferred to another boat, and it was on that boat that he was killed. That shook me up pretty bad. I'm getting over it now.

There is one thing I want to bring up. Mom, this is to you. With your letters and your tapes that you have sent, they have helped me so much, and they've got that touch of home and touch of love to me. I always enjoy the tapes because when you sign off, I never know what to expect, and you always give those words of comfort and of love, and they have meant so much to me. I always look forward to getting in from an operation to hear a tape or read a letter. Like I said, they have done so much for me. It's so reassuring to know that there is someone at home who cares, is thinking about me, and praying about me. I love you very deeply for it. Mother, you made my year so much easier. I'm sorry that I have not been able to send those words of love I'm sure you wanted so often. I just wasn't able to. I wanted to, but time and circumstances didn't let that work out that way.

This tape is almost done. I'm not. As I said earlier, it is my last one, but I'll be sending some quick letters. Happiness to me is to know that I'm so close to coming home, and I feel so safe now. Wish I could say that about the guys still out there. Say hi to everybody, and tell them, "The kid's coming home!" What can I say? I'm feeling pretty good right now, and I can hardly contain myself. It won't be long. Next time you hear my voice, I will be in person.

Friday the 13th, Dec 1968

It's Friday the 13th. I will never let anybody try to tell me or convince me that this date could be a bad day. What do they know about waking up in your favorite bedroom before the sun has come up and you will be experiencing a day of ultimate freedom? What would they know about what the last year has been like?

Three weeks ago, I got off a boat of death and destruction. It had been my home for so long. When the time of relief occurred, several of my closest friends and boat crew members were still at the most infamous location, the Crossroads. They had headed there knowing they would probably be involved in a firefight and might not get to go home as a living being.

After they returned, we were sent to Dong Tam. At Dong Tam, we created a very special and unique military uniform. We took the green fatigues of stateside Army bases, black stateside boots, a camouflage beret, and name tags (name and branch of service type) of blue with gold piping letters. We added our unit patches and awarded military ribbons for finishing touches. We were looking good.

Even Charlie, the Viet Cong, gave us an explosive send-off. Charlie decided to mortar the Dong Tam Army Base during our last night. We were in the Navy barracks with a bunch of newbies. The mortars started hitting, and the newbies started yelling and screaming. Then they ran for the bunkers to hide from the mortars, but the 11 of us (from the original 120+) with 14 documented Purple Hearts (and numerous unreported combat injuries) from the boats remained in our bunks and laughed. What's the worst that could happen?

When we arrived at Travis Air Force Base, it was already dark and cold, so the typical anti-war, wimpy, self-seeking protesters who could not handle any level of discomfort were not there. The four of us (Robert, Rodger-Dodger, Gomer, and I) jumped into a taxi and headed for the San Francisco Airport. When we arrived, we agreed to meet up after we had purchased our tickets home. I went to Southwest Airlines to purchase a ticket to Ontario, California, and they said the flight was leaving, but they would delay its departure since I had no baggage to check (I was just carrying an overnight case with the flag from our boat), and I could run to get on it. I ran as fast as I could, got aboard, and sat down by an Air Force sergeant. We talked, had a few drinks, and then he offered me a ride to my home.

Well, here I am at home. Last night, Jacquie, Mom, Dad, and John were waiting for a phone call to let them know when I was getting home. But instead, I knocked at the door, and they let me in.

Friday the 13th is not a bad day. The sun is coming up, I'm looking at the valley of Riverside, California, and all is good. I know there are many crossroads ahead, and it makes me think of King David and his songs, especially Psalm 124, and I must say it in my own words:

If it had not been the Lord who was on my side, how could I say,
"If it had not been the Lord who was on my side, when men rose
*   up against us,*
They would have swallowed us up quick, when their wrath was
*   kindled against us.*
The waters would have overwhelmed us, the stream would have
*   gone over our soul.*
Blessed be the Lord who has not given us as a prey to their teeth.
My soul has escaped as a bird out of the snare of the fowlers; the
*   snare is broken, and I have escaped.*
My help is in the name of the Lord who made heaven and earth."

A few minutes after I got home

The Cua Viet Experience
(the Rest of the Story)

The following description about Task Force Clearwater (river mine-sweepers) is from *Upriver to Hue and Dong Ha: The U.S. Navy's War in I Corps, Vietnam, 1967–1970*, a thesis by Jonathan Blackshear Chavanne, 2011, Texas A&M University, College Station, Texas:

> The brown water mission is one that has proven both important but transitory in the history of the U.S. Navy, rising and falling according to the maritime and strategic needs of the time. During the Vietnam War it played a vital but often overlooked role, and of the major brown water task forces, Clearwater has been the least remembered. Yet this river force played a key role far out of proportion to its size and place in historical memory. Far from a footnote to history, the men and boats of this small brown water fleet are inseparable parts of America's searing experience in Vietnam. Strategically located on the sandy south bank of the river's mouth, Cua Viet was a dreary place, more resembling a ramshackle boomtown than a U.S. Navy installation. The base expanded considerably from its founding in the summer of 1967, and in the words of one naval officer had been transformed from a beautiful, white, unoccupied, sandy beach into an ugly, but thriving, cantonment of plywood huts and mess halls.

Cua Viet is grim, dirty, dusty, gritty, isolated, dangerous, and the perfect place to not be bored.

Cua Viet, March 1970 – What Am I Doing Here?

It is normal to think that a year of combat in Vietnam would be enough excitement and misery for a lifetime. Yet after five months aboard a ship, Navy life had become extremely boring and mundane. Because I was addicted to adrenaline, I could not handle my assigned tasks. I had two simple assignments when the ship was out to sea and sometimes even in port. One assignment was to watch deck crew seamen chip paint. I was even scolded for chipping paint while supervising paint chippers. My second assignment was to stand on the bridge of the ship and be ready to conduct voice communication with other entities, if needed. The ship primarily used teletype communication, or they would use the old standby of flags and signal lights. I did not know how to do any of those.

The Navy had a simple personnel rule that allowed a Vietnam veteran to request a return to that country, and the sailor could not be refused. On Memorial Day weekend, 1969, I made my request. After watching a US astronaut land on the moon, I packed my bags and returned to Vietnam. Within days, I was at a place called Cua Viet.

I have been in Cua Viet now for about eight months. It gets bombarded day and night from NVA artillery and mortar fire. I am a boat captain of a minesweeper on this river. Our daily job is a suicide mission from the little base at the mouth of the river to the ramp at Dong Ha and then back, checking the rivers for mines. Every day I think about the friends I lost two years ago when a Tango boat was blown out of the water. We find mines very frequently, maybe not daily but several in a week can be typical. Some we can see floating and will detonate them with gunfire or concussion grenades. Some we cannot see, but the concussion grenades still cause them to explode. Some we find in our minesweeping gear. When we pull the gear out of the water, we have UDT or SEALs come to disarm them. Others are found (detonated) either by the water pressure at the bow of the boat or from the water disturbance at the stern of the boat. The ones that are not found by the already mentioned ways are the dangerous ones. They are either detonated remotely by someone on shore or by the boat making direct contact with the mine. That is called "finding it the hard way." I have already found a couple the "hard way." It is logical for the military to reason that losing a small boat with a small crew is cost-effective compared to losing a large boat loaded with military supplies and a large crew.

The morning started off as usual with minesweeping up to Dong Ha and then returning to our base camp at the mouth of the river. After the routine excursion, an assignment was given to transport an army truck and trailer with a few soldiers back up to the ramp at Dong Ha. Simple. Easy. No big deal. Something to do. Take six soldiers and their equipment up the river. Only four men will get to their destination.

As I regained consciousness, I realized I was swimming, and I didn't know why. I quickly remembered that I had been looking at an object in the river. It appeared to be some kind of a broom. As memory returned and I reached the riverbank, it was second nature to look out to the middle of the river. The bottom of my boat could be seen sticking up and out of the water. Within moments, two other sailors and four army soldiers also arrived at the bank. We had been victims of a very big mine found the hard way.

> King Solomon says in Ecclesiastes 3: 1–11:
> "To everything there is a season, and a time to every purpose
>   under the heaven:
> A time to be born, and a time to die; a time to plant, and a time
>   to pluck up that which is planted;
> A time to kill, and a time to heal; a time to break down, and a
>   time to build up;
> A time to weep, and a time to laugh; a time to mourn, and a
>   time to dance; . . .
> A time to love, and a time to hate; a time of war, and a time of
>   peace . . .
> He hath made every thing beautiful in his time."

Mason Williams, of Classical Gas fame, wrote and sings a 30-second tune called "Life Song." The words are perfect for this situation because he describes life as beautiful, gay, and "the perfect thing to pass the time away."

Cua Viet, March 1970 – The Business Plan

"If you do that again, I will make sure you spend time at Leavenworth," is what the full-bird-combat-infantry Marine colonel told us when he dismissed that case. "That case" had been my business plan that was very successful. It all started when I noticed that the officers were allowed to have hard liquor in their underground sandbag bunker, completely safe from any and all enemy artillery or mortar attacks. The enlisted men were not allowed to have any hard liquor, and it was very hard to obtain any kind of beer, cold or warm.

When we traveled upstream to Dong Ha, by the time we got to the ramp, it would be warm, and we would be thirsty. The kids would come out to us as we beached our boats and brought in our minesweeping gear. After bringing the gear on board to clear it of mines, we would trade with the Vietnamese kids. They enjoyed getting a pack of cigarettes and would gladly give us ice-cold, US-made colas. They weren't allowed to have our American-made cigarettes, and they also were not allowed to be in possession of those soda cans. We weren't supposed to get anything from the Vietnamese people that should be US government property. We also weren't allowed to use US money, military money, or US-supplied property to obtain anything from the Vietnamese. Basically, we were dabbling in what is called the black market, illegal traffic or trade in officially controlled or scarce commodities.

Some of the crew members decided that they might enjoy some whiskey. We decided to ask the kids whether it was possible to get a bottle. The kids told us they would get a bottle of rice whiskey and trade it for a carton of cigarettes. We got the cigarettes, took them upriver the next day, and came back with our cherished bottle. A couple of Marine soldiers happened to see us enjoying our drinks and asked how much it would cost them to get a similar quantity. We threw out the price of $10, and they all agreed it was a fair amount. Cartons of cigarettes cost $1.10 at the ship's outpost store (the store was the size of a big closet), and they had ample cartons of Lucky Strikes. Nobody would buy those cigarettes because they were so old that when a pack was opened, all you could find was yellow, shriveled, dried-up cigarettes.

Obtaining cigarettes, rice whiskey, and Marine money was easy, but getting the money back home was a little bit of a problem. Every couple of days, I would have the equivalent of a month's income. The Navy knew how much money I should have, and the military had many ways of reducing profits from any kind of black market operation. The military countermeasure for illegal profiteering primarily focused on in-country activities. The military was not worried about the ships that were out in the ocean.

As a boat captain and unit leader of several boats, I was allowed to go out to sea whenever time was available to test-fire and train crew members with weapons. When we were at sea, the small ships in the area invited us to come alongside so they could show off their hospitality. They would gladly serve us a meal, open up the post office and the ship's store, and do anything else they possibly could to accommodate any of our wants and needs. Therefore, I could buy money orders to send home that were out of the in-country process of money control. I could also purchase ample cigarettes on board and use them for trading material upriver to get those sweet bottles of whiskey.

What a business plan! This should be smooth sailing.

Living life in Cua Viet, 1970

Cua Viet, March 1970 – Going Out of Business Sail

The OIC (officer in charge) is one of a kind. He prefers to stay down and inside the underground bunker all day. When he comes up to the real world, he enjoys finding fault with what we do. He is a Navy lieutenant who has not learned very many basic leadership skills, but he is in charge. He seems to enjoy taking the wind out of everyone's sails and has gotten wind that there are many Marine soldiers who have access to whiskey. He has apparently used his military intelligence training and skills to deduce that a possible source of the whiskey might be from the minesweeping boats and their daily chores.

He shows up at the boat docks one morning and wants to ride on the minesweeping excursion. We believe he's there to see us make a transaction with the kids at the Dong Ha ramp. He rides on my boat since I am the senior leader, and as we approached the ramp, I get him involved in a conversation. Meanwhile, the other boat begins giving hand signals to the kids on shore that there will not be any trading today. We beach and pull in the gear, but as we are bringing the gear onto the boat, the Lieutenant is up at the ramp trading a pack of cigarettes for a cold Coca-Cola. We sailors looked at each other with questions in our eyes and slight smiles on our lips.

After the return trip to Cua Viet, we decide to suspend our business operation for a few days. At the end of a business suspension, we gear up for business again and start our usual trading of cartons of cigarettes for those succulent bottles of rice whiskey. The wind blows smoothly and gently for several days until we hear the wind rush of a bubble cockpit helicopter. The little thing flies directly over us as we are passing cartons for bottles between the hands of kids and us.

The face of our esteemed leader is staring down at us, and we know we are doomed. When we arrive back at our home base, we are met by a Marine escort detail. The leader of the detail informs us that we are being escorted to the Marine commander for a Captain's Mast (prelim for a court martial). The full-bird-combat-infantry Marine Colonel has the meanest, toughest face of anyone I have ever seen.

Someone reads the list of charges that are being brought up against us. The Colonel's graveled voice growls, "Are there any questions?" I respond with a simple and timid "Yes, Sir" and then ask, "If someone traded a pack of cigarettes for a cold Coca-Cola, would the charges be basically the same?" He replies that the charges would be basically the same. I then point at our Navy Lieutenant and say, "That is what he did." The other sailors are nodding their heads in agreement. "If you do that again, I will make sure you spend time at Leavenworth" was his response. Case dismissed.

The business is now *Gone with the Wind*.

Cua Viet, March 1970 – Singing in the Rain

There must be a storm brewing somewhere out in the Pacific Ocean. Apparently, it is typhoon size in intensity because the waves at the mouth of the river are hitting at about 30+ feet in height. Traveling up and down the river for minesweeping is not a problem, but I've been told that I now need to take a boat to Da Nang. Normally, repairs are done here, but the military is starting to shut down this base and plans to turn it over to the Vietnamese, so the broken boats will be returned to the home base in Da Nang. This tasking will provide a break from the developing work schedule. We currently man and operate the boats from sunrise to sunset every day. Breakfast is eaten before going down to the boats. After the day of boating chores, we must guard the boat facilities at night. Basically, the schedule is becoming 36 hours on duty and 12 off.

The boat that needs to be returned is called an LCM 6. It has two engines and two screws to propel it. A major problem with this boat is that one engine is not working. Therefore, in order to drive the boat straight, you rev up the non-broken engine and turn the helm wheel toward the side with the good engine, similar to turning into a skid. I will need to drive this boat straight into huge, oncoming waves. What fun that will be! Another problem is that a non-working engine creates a situation of only one bilge pump. There may be issues with water spilling into the well deck that cannot be expelled fast enough. Did I mention it's raining cats and dogs (i.e., cougars and St. Bernards)?

When I get out into the ocean, a tow rope will be tied to the boat. The boat will then be dragged by a larger boat all the way to the Da Nang Harbor. Easy trip. As we head out to sea, the two crewmen position themselves up on the bow ramp so they can look over the waves and tell me what to do. When we crest one gigantic wave, it becomes cartoonish. The bow drops, and it appears that a crewman is suspended in air. He then drops into the well deck and breaks an arm. Now it's time to turn the boat around and head back into the Cua Viet base so he can be taken by medevac to a hospital ship. The 50-foot-plus boat then becomes the world's biggest surfboard. It is fun riding monstrous North Shore style waves in such a crazy way.

We get the crewman taken care of and get back out in the ocean. About the time the tow rope is being passed, the other engine quits working. The tow boat has to fight the storm, and we have no communication with it. By the time it gets turned around and headed toward us, we are drifting north into a place called North Vietnam. This is not a Sunday afternoon drive in sunny Southern California.

The darkness of night arrives at about the same time the tow boat does, and our second engine starts working again. The crewman ties me into the cox'n flat and heads for the well deck. He didn't want me to get washed overboard during the night. At sunrise, we arrive in Da Nang. The boat has taken on so much water that it is sinking. As I drive the boat into the harbor, I head straight to a beach area and run the ramp up onto the shore as the back end goes under water. I walk off the boat and head for the enlisted club. No one said I had to turn in any paperwork or tell anybody about the boat. I will now have to deal with getting back to Cua Viet. But first, the enlisted club. This is not the time to dry out.

Cua Viet, March 1970 – Purple Haze

Purple haze, purple haze. I must recount the last few days of how I got messed up in so many ways.

Yesterday, I arrived in Da Nang, dropped off my sinking boat, and lost my crewman. I headed toward the enlisted club but might have found my way to the SEALs quarters where refreshments were available 24/7. I imbibed because they invited. I was given 72 hours to take a boat to Da Nang and get back to Cua Viet. I used 12 hours officially and 24 hours personally getting into a purple haze. Now it's time to get back up north. I go to the base's gate and start hitching rides. At sunset I arrive at the Dong Ha ramp. I have no weapon, and I have no knowledge of where American resources are. I do know that this territory has a high concentration of NVA troops, enemy sympathizers, and other assorted Viet Cong. In other words, this is enemy-friendly territory. There is a US military regulation that all boats of any shape, size, form, ownership, or purpose must be off the river before it becomes dark. As I get down to the ramp, I see the last boat that has left Dong Ha heading toward Cua Viet going around the curve out of sight and out of visual and audio reach. I am in enemy territory and basically vulnerable to any enemy activity. As I stand there feeling inadequate and ashamed, a teenage boy confronts me. It just so happens I recognize this boy (really a young man). He is one of the youngsters who greet us every morning at the Dong Ha ramp. You could say he has been a significant business partner. Although he only speaks very limited English, we manage to establish the fact that I am up the creek without a paddle. He realizes that I need to get down the creek but can't. He communicates in broken English that I should go home with him, so I follow him to his house, which is really a one-room hooch.

His home has Papa San, Mama San, and some siblings. They invite me in, and we share dinner and an evening of laughter and pure enjoyment. I don't speak their language, and they don't speak mine, but we could speak the language of acceptance, enjoyment, laughter, and overall camaraderie. As the evening winds down, the teenage boy shows me where to sleep. It is a mat on the ground. Papa San digs through his personal belongings and produces a relic of a rusty, worn-out rifle. It looks like a weapon from WW I, and if it were to be fired, it might explode in the shooter's hands. In broken English, the young man explains that Papa San will guard the house from the enemy.

It should be noted that at my base camp of Cua Viet, my fellow patriots have played a game for months. The primary focus of that game has been to try to wake me up; that is, to touch me before I say anything to them. I sleep combat-ready lightly. I don't like surprises or being caught off-guard, and no one has been able to touch me before I react to their proximity. At this point in life, I have spent 20 months in hostile territory with expected disruptions, but on this night, I sleep the deepest sleep of any of my many days in Vietnam.

At sunrise, the young man awakens me. Papa San is standing by with his rusty relic and a huge grin on his face. The teenage business partner manages an explanation about the VC and NVA looking for me all night but not being successful about finding me.

At sunrise, it dawns on me that people can communicate in spite of language barriers, that people can enjoy common emotions, that people share commonality that goes beyond words. My Vietnam boy savior escorts me down to the ramp, and by the time we get there, I see a US Navy minesweeping boat coming from Cua Viet headed for the ramp. They will get me back to where I belong.

The CrossRoads Diaries Epilogue – 30 to 50 Years Later

Ain't Nuttin

"Ain't nuttin but a thang,"
But what about the pain?
"Ain't nuttin but a thang,"
But what about the rain?
It pours, it anews, it refreshes!
Rain on me, rain on my ashes!
Put the fire out, wet it down!
The phrase in Nam is renowned
It's the response to pain!
"Ain't nuttin but a thang."

One year after arriving home in 1970, I became a member of a Southern California police department. A few years later, the residual stresses and strains of my Vietnam service and the current job impacted my marriage to Jacquie. I was still addicted to an adrenalin rush. After 10 years of rebellion toward my God because of the firefight on August 16, 1968, I reaffirmed that He had sent His Son to die for my sins. A second marriage occurred that also ended because of the same factors as the first. I drifted in and out of several professions and found myself back in Army boot camp at the age of 34. After six years of Army service, I received a medical retirement for PTSD. During Army service time, I remarried. As of the time of writing this book, the marriage has survived and will do so until the Lord calls one of us home.

During the middle of 1997, the phone started ringing between Frank, Gomer, and me. Gomer had tracked down Frank's phone number and mine and started calling us. We then contacted each other. During the phone conversations, it was discovered that no one had found Robert or Rodger-Dodger. Gomer expressed his belief, because of information he had somehow discovered, that the two of them had taken their own lives because of depression (from PTSD).

Frank explained to us that the fingers we had picked up from the deck and wrapped in his mangled hand had been reattached and were somewhat functional. Frank and I met up during an afternoon in a Flagstaff, Arizona, restaurant. He had some significant scarring on his face and had to wear sunglasses most of the time, even inside. We sat down in a deserted dining area and shared our memories for several hours. Our talking stopped for a few moments, and we looked around and discovered that the dining area had filled with customers, and everyone had been listening to us.

During the fall of 1997, I attended a Mobile Riverine Force Association reunion. It was a gathering of soldiers and sailors who had lived and fought alongside each other in the Mekong Delta. Stories and memories were affirmed, friendships were rekindled, and the Brotherhood was strengthened.

During the remainder of 1997 through June 1998, Gomer and I talked many times. Gomer would call at any time of the day or night to express his thoughts and feelings about our time and bonds in Vietnam. During the year of those phone calls, I was having major issues with PTSD. Gomer also had PTSD issues, but they were minor compared to the cancer (agent orange–related) issues he was having. He had lost both legs and was basically in hospice. He helped me get through what I was dealing with, but I could only offer a listening ear to what he was experiencing. He died in June 1998. RIP, my dear friend.

I have been married to a wonderful wife, Sandy, for more than 35 years. I've helped raise three daughters and feel blessed to have had a varied and interesting life. An additional blessing came in 2016 when College of the Ozarks provided me an opportunity to return to Vietnam. It was a time of healing.

Death Gives Life

Some are alive when they are close to death
And death brings a life of its own.
My Savior died so that we could live
And I owe my life to Him alone.
To live or die, as Paul once said,
Brings us to life when we are dead.
Choose to live a life beyond death
And experience riches beyond wealth.

My boat, *Tango 91-4*, during a combat operation. The pictured flag is now part of the College of the Ozarks' Vietnam Memorabilia Collection.

Return to Vietnam 2016
By Brittany Hedges (née Allee)

Today was a day of exploring and reminiscing. We enjoyed a cruise on the Cua Viet River in the morning and toured the Vinh Moc Tunnels, which were used by the NVA to fight American forces. We then visited Hien Luong Bridge that spans the DMZ (demilitarized zone) that acted as the boundary between North and South Vietnam during the war. Although all these excursions were fascinating and exciting, my favorite part of the day was our cruise on the Cua Viet River. Tom Center, my hero, my veteran, and my friend, cruised on the very same river 47 years ago but under much different circumstances.

Tom served two tours of duty during the Vietnam War, from 1967–1970. He was assigned to the Mobile Riverine Task Force on his first tour, which was a water-based joint task force of Army and Navy units that operated throughout the Mekong River Delta. Tom was specifically a part of River Squadron 9's River Division 91. He was a coxswain (the steersman of the boat) on an Armored Troop Carrier, *Tango 91-4*. His unit's job was to search and destroy the enemy along the rivers as well as transport American soldiers. He was involved in around 100 firefights, and by the end of his first tour, Tom's unit had suffered an 80 percent casualty rate, something I cannot comprehend.

On his second tour, Tom was stationed on the Cua Viet River, which is the northernmost river in South Vietnam, very close to the DMZ. His job was to conduct daily minesweeping operations to ensure it was safe for resupply crafts to deliver their goods. Tom said, "Minesweeping was like going on a suicide mission every day."

As we cruised the river, I saw the memories flood back into Tom's mind. He believed he would never be back on the Cua Viet River again, yet here we were. I watched him relax on the river where he once feared for his life and was reminded of a poem Tom wrote and shared with us earlier this morning.

The scars of life can tell a story,
And most scars do not bring praise or glory,
Some can bring peace, and some bring worry,
Some scars are seen, stories are told,
Some scars hidden, stories on hold,
Some scars change timid to bold,
Some scars make a puzzle unfold,
Some scars leave damage like mold,
A few scars are more precious than gold.

Reflecting on the poem, I realized that all veterans carry scars from the war; however, when I looked at Tom this morning as we cruised the river and landed at the same spot he had docked many times before, I realize that Tom's scars have healed. They aren't gone, and he will never forget they are there, but he is whole. I am blessed to know Tom Center. He is a hero. He is a man of God. And he is someone I will always admire.

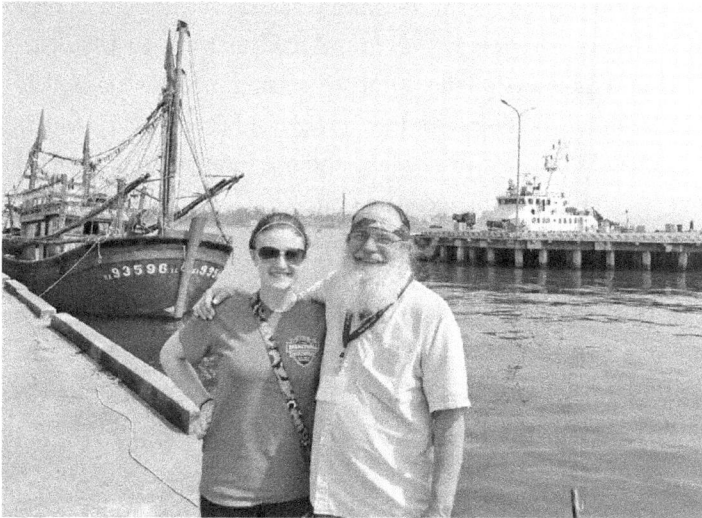

Brittany and Tom at the Cua Viet dock, March 2016

College of the Ozarks Patriotic Education Program

The College of the Ozarks Patriotic Education Program was founded to reinforce the patriotic goal of the college. That goal is "to encourage an understanding of American heritage, civic responsibilities, love of country, and a willingness to defend it."

The Patriotic Education Travel Program provides once-in-a-lifetime opportunities for students to travel with veterans to historic battle sites all over the world. Veterans share their experiences with students and ensure that the sacrifices of our nation's heroes will never be forgotten. The three objectives of the Patriotic Education Program are as follows:

1. Educate the students about the sacrifices paid for our freedoms
2. Commemorate the fallen
3. Honor the veterans

The Program began in 2009 with 10 veterans and 20 students traveling to England and Normandy for the 65th Anniversary of D-Day. Subsequent trips have been taken to the battlefields of Operation Market-Garden in Holland; the Battle of the Bulge in Belgium and Luxembourg; Okinawa, Iwo Jima, and Hiroshima; Kasserine Pass in Tunisia; and Monte Cassino and Anzio in Italy. In October 2010, students and veterans of the 101st Airborne Division traveled to Normandy, Holland, Belgium, and Germany. In March 2011, students and Pacific veterans traveled to Hawaii, and another group returned in December for the 70th anniversary of the attack on Pearl Harbor. Additionally, the college has made trips back to Normandy and the Battle of the Bulge; the Philippines; a Holocaust trip to Germany, Austria, and Poland; and in December 2012, to Guadalcanal.

In May 2013, College of the Ozarks students traveled with Army Air Corps, Navy Armed Guards, and Merchant Marine veterans to England to commemorate the 70th anniversary of the Air War and the Battle of the Atlantic. In October 2013, the program toured with Korean War veterans to commemorate the 60th anniversary of the Korean War Armistice. In June 2014, students attended the 70th Anniversary Commemoration of D-Day. On this trip, eight D-Day veterans accompanied students to Normandy, Belgium, and Luxembourg for visits to the Battle of the Bulge historic sites. For 12 days in September and October 2014, 12 College of the Ozarks students accompanied 12 Vietnam War veterans for the inaugural Patriotic Education trip to Vietnam. They journeyed together visiting places such as Saigon, the Mekong Delta, the la Drang Valley, Da Nang, Khe Sanh, Hue, and Hanoi.

In May 2015, students went to Guam and Japan with Marine, Navy, and Army Air Corps World War II veterans who fought in the Marianas and conducted the bombing campaign over Japan. In October 2015, 13 College of the Ozarks students accompanied five US veterans on a Cold War Commemorative Tour. During this 10-day period, the group visited key historical sites in Europe from the Cold War era, including Germany, the Czech Republic, and Austria.

Since 2009, the college has taken a total of 23 trips, four of which have been to Vietnam. Approximately 150 veterans and nearly 350 students have participated in these patriotic programs.

All these journeys have proved to be life-changing experiences for the College of the Ozarks students. They not only learn about history firsthand from veterans but also grow to love and appreciate those who served. The students who attended these trips have returned with renewed respect for veterans and have dramatically increased their love for their country.

A Closing Comment from the Author

The Patriotic Program of the College of the Ozarks is a worthwhile effort to educate the young while helping veterans heal from emotional scars.

Any contribution to that program will be beneficial to many more vets, as it has been for me.

The author can be contacted at:
Tom Center
PO Box 52
Kirbyville, MO 65679
tango91four@gmail.com

About the Author

After Tom Center graduated from high school at the age of 17, his mother reluctantly signed for him to join the Navy so he could avoid serving in Vietnam. However, he volunteered for combat duty from 1967 to 1968 with the joint Army-Navy Mobile Riverine Force in Vietnam's Mekong Delta. From 1969 to 1970, he served a second tour of duty in Vietnam, traversing the Cua Viet River in the northern part of South Vietnam, looking for mines. Thirteen years later, he rejoined the military and then received a medical retirement. After serving in Vietnam, Tom graduated from the Los Angeles Police Academy, served as a patrolman and a school resource officer, taught high school, and became a military intelligence instructor and a safety instructor for OSHA and MSHA. He has degrees in law enforcement, sociology, and education. He has been happily married since 1983.

www.ingramcontent.com/pod-product-compliance
Lightning Source LLC
Chambersburg PA
CBHW071753090426
42737CB00012B/1805